FINANCING HIGHER EDUCATION IN A GLOBAL ECONOMY

RICHARD E. ANDERSON

JOEL W. MEYERSON

Sponsored by the
NATIONAL CENTER FOR POSTSECONDARY GOVERNANCE AND FINANCE

American Council on Education   Macmillan Publishing Company
New York
Collier Macmillan Publishers
London

Macmillan Publishing Company
866 Third Avenue, New York, N.Y. 10022

Collier Macmillan Canada, Inc.

Library of Congress Catalog Card Number: 89-35925

Printed in the United States of America

printing number
1 2 3 4 5 6 7 8 9 10

Library of Congress Cataloging in Publication Data

Financing higher education in a global economy / Richard E. Anderson,
Joel W. Meyerson ; sponsored by the National Center for Postsecondary Governance and Finance.
    p.   cm.—(American Council on Education/Macmillan series in higher education)
    Bibliography: p.
    ISBN 0-02-900965-0
    1. Universities and colleges—United States—Finance.
    2. Education, Higher—Economic aspects—United States.   3. Higher education
and state—United States.   4. Economic development—Effect of education on.
    I. Anderson, Richard E., 1943–   .   II. Meyerson, Joel W., 1951–   .
    III. National Center for Postsecondary Governance and Finance (U.S.)   IV. Ameri-
can Council on Education. V. Series.
    LB2342.F515   1990
    3379.1'214'0973—dc20   89-35925
                                                                                       CIP

CONTENTS

CONTENTS

PREFACE

Few changes are having a greater impact on our lives than increasing globalization, particularly of the world's economies. Ironically, an important impetus for growing internationalization has been American higher education, which has produced a steady stream of innovation—new ideas and technologies, new ways of processing and communicating information—that has changed the way the world works. Having helped change the world, American colleges and universities must now adapt to new circumstances. High on the list of challenges is ensuring that institutions have adequate resources to respond to future change and to remain competitive.

To help explore the complexities and challenges of the emerging business environment, the Forum For College Financing recently conducted a national symposium on "Financing Higher Education in a Global Economy." This book is the result of the papers presented at that meeting. The Forum (a research project of the National Center for Postsecondary Governance and Finance), brought together "thought-leaders" from the academic and business community to discuss new approaches to college financing. Senior officers from institutions such as Boston College, Columbia University, and Stanford University examined new strategies for financing instruction and research. Business leaders from Coopers & Lybrand, Goldman Sachs, and Standard and Poor analyzed debt policy, taxable financing, credit enhancement, and other issues. The result was a new perspective on how institutions of higher education will have to finance their operations in the future—as well as the unforeseen challenges that lay ahead.

Gail Franck and Doug Wofford of the Forum staff contributed significantly to the success of the symposium and this book and their assistance is gratefully acknowledged. Coopers & Lybrand serves as technical advisor to the Forum.

Richard E. Anderson
Joel W. Meyerson

v

CONTRIBUTORS

Richard E. Anderson is a co-director of the Forum for College Financing. Dr. Anderson is also a Professor at Teachers College, Columbia University, where he directs a joint program with the Graduate School of Business. He has written or edited six books and monographs on higher education finance including *Finance and Effectiveness* and *The Costs and Finance of Adult Education and Training*. Dr. Anderson has served as a consultant to a number of colleges, states, and to the federal government.

Frank B. Campanella has been Executive Vice President of Boston College since 1973. Prior to that he was a Professor of Management at Boston College. His books include *The Measurement of Portfolio Risk Exposure* and *Venture Capital: A Guide for New Enterprises*.

Robert T. Forrester is a Partner at Coopers & Lybrand and coordinates the firm's New England higher education practice. He also works nationwide with colleges, universities, and other non-profit organizations. Mr. Forrester is a national authority on accounting and auditing standards, and chairs an AICPA task force on audits of federal programs at nonprofit organizations. In addition to several articles on accounting and financial reporting, he has recently authored NACUBO's *Handbook on Debt Management for Colleges and Universities*.

Daniel Heimowitz is Vice President and Managing Director of Structured Ratings in the Municipal Department of Moody's Investor Service. Mr. Heimowitz is a member of

Dun & Bradstreet's Information Resource Coordinating Council, the Municipal Analysts Group of New York, and the Municipal Forum. He also serves on the Public Securities Association's Research and Education Committee and on the Financial Reporting Task Force of the Government Accounting Standards Board.

Arthur J. Kalita is President of Morgan Bank of Canada. Prior to that he was Managing Director of J.P. Morgan Securities, Inc., and Senior Vice President of Morgan Guarantee Trust Co. Before joining the Morgan Bank he served as the Executive Director of the Public Securities Association. Mr. Kalita has served on a number of professional committees including the Committee on Municipal Affairs of the Association of the Bar of the City of New York, and the Steering Committee on Municipal Disclosure of the Government Finance Officers Association and the National Association of Bond Lawyers.

Anthony D. Knerr is president of the Publishing Group. Prior to assuming that position he was Executive Vice President for Finance and Treasurer of Columbia University. He has also served as Special Assistant to the President for Budget and Planning at Yale and Vice Chancellor for Budget and Planning at the City University of New York. He is treasurer of a Franco-American institution in Paris, Vice President of a settlement house, and Chairman of the steering committee of the New York Center for Visual History.

William F. Massy is Vice President of Finance at Stanford University and is a professor in the University's Colleges of Education and Business. Dr. Massy has consulted with and served as director to a large number of corporations and non-profit organizations across the country. Dr. Massy has written numerous books, articles, and papers on business subjects and on higher education management. His major publications include *Planning Models for Colleges and*

Universities (with Hopkins) and *The Economics of Endowed Universities.*

Joel W. Meyerson is co-director of the Forum for College Financing and a partner at Coopers & Lybrand, where he directs their higher education practice. He has authored or edited several recent books, including *Financing Higher Education: Strategies After Tax Reform* (with Richard E. Anderson), *Strategic Decision-Making: Key Questions and Indicators for Trustees* (AGB), and *Alternative Approaches to Tuition Financing* (NACUBO). Joel edits the *Higher Education Management Newsletter*, published by Coopers & Lybrand, and the Agenda Priorities column in *AGB Reports.*

Douglas Wofford is director of information services of Communicorp Inc. and previously was a research associate with the Forum for College Financing Alternatives. He was previously Director of Admissions at McMurry College in Texas.

1

A CHANGING
NATIONAL
ENVIRONMENT

RICHARD E. ANDERSON
JOEL W. MEYERSON

MANY of the assumptions that underlie our belief in national greatness are being questioned. We are taking a long, introspective look at our capabilities, and contemplating our strength and vitality in economic, military, and other terms. The questions are often disturbing. Have we slipped? Is a new economic order emerging? Where will we fit in? Will we fade from the scene or re-emerge as a more adaptive, nimble competitor?

Increasingly, attention has focused on our economic situation. While still the "economic engine of the world," we have sputtered a little of late. Relative prosperity, low unemployment, and economic growth belie unprecedented trade and budget deficits, loss of foreign and domestic markets, and a more volatile financial system. Clearly, we are no longer the economic powerhouse we once were. The prospect of losing control of our economic—and national—destiny to foreign governments and corporations, once unthinkable, is now hotly debated. How should we respond? How do we regain national prominence?

Increasingly, people are turning to our institutions of higher learning for answers to these questions. They are seeking responses that go beyond scholarly projections and analyses of our role in the world. They are looking at colleges and universities as a crucial part of the equation that defines a competitive, sustainable economy. In this role, colleges are expected to create knowledge through basic research and innovation, as well as educate future members of a motivated and intellectually adept work force. To accomplish these goals, higher education institutions themselves must be financially viable and secure. For all but a few institutions, however, this is an objective difficult to achieve. Many institutions have been rocked by an erratic national higher education policy, unfavorable tax legislation, falling public esteem, rising capital requirements, and a shrinking college-age population.

This book examines several important aspects of financing higher education in a global economy. The chapters summarized below focus on financing those components of the academic mission linked to national prosperity—research and instruction—as well as improving overall institutional financial vigor.

THE ECONOMY AND HIGHER EDUCATION
by Richard E. Anderson, *Director,*
Forum for College Financing

In the first chapter, Richard E. Anderson explores the macroeconomic trends that shape the U.S. economy and affect higher education.

The rate of growth in the Gross National Product (GNP), which is a measure of the economy's productivity, has been trending downward since the 1970s, and appears even more stagnant when corrected for the number of workers. On the other hand, consumption by the federal government (and to a lesser extent by citizens) has increased significantly, leading to a federal budget deficit that has consistently exceeded 3 percent of GNP since 1982. The United States has propped up its standard of

2

living further by importing more goods than are exported, creating an extraordinarily high trade deficit.

The size, magnitude, and persistence of these twin deficits hinder prospects for future growth in the economy. The United States has gone from the world's largest creditor to its largest debtor in just a few years. The consequences of the deficits besides debt, include relatively high interest rates, a weak dollar, and a weakened infrastructure. Economic analysts disagree about the long-term effects. The best-case scenario calls for modest growth, while the worst calls for worldwide economic contraction.

Because of the budget deficit, federal assistance to higher education is not likely to increase. In addition, the industry's favorable tax status might be threatened. State governments, constrained by the laggard economy, will not be able to absorb federal shortfalls and may call for greater accountability from public institutions. A recession would constrain government support of higher education even further.

Low family income levels and savings rates may depress enrollments of U.S. students, but a weak dollar will encourage foreign student enrollments. Unpredictable capital markets will increase financing costs and may make investing more hazardous. Inflation will affect higher education with particular severity, but a recession might spur enrollments, especially at public institutions.

Public policy makers will try to respond proactively to the forthcoming economic trends and events. The development of more research or production parks near universities, increased university-business cooperation, and an additional demand for foreign studies and modern languages are likely. In the changing economy, higher education leaders must balance carefully the institution's mission to provide a broad-based education with societal demands to produce a highly trained work force.

3

FINANCING RESEARCH
by William F. Massy, *Vice President for Business and Finance and Professor of Business Administration,* Stanford University

Research funding is currently under siege on two fronts: the financing of indirect costs under Office of Management and Budget (OMB) Circular A-21 and the shrinking pool of research dollars.

A-21 currently uses the "averaging principle," under which if sponsored research represents X percent of total institutional activity, then the institution's indirect costs are reimbursed up to X percent. The process of negotiating indirect cost recovery rates among government representatives, university administrators, and faculty researchers has become more complex and divisive under A-21. Not all researchers, who usually obtain and administer the grants, fully understand and support A-21's numerous rules. Rather, the system encourages some "free-riders," or researchers who are not motivated to recover all indirect costs on behalf of their institutions.

Moreover, empirical data suggests that the averaging principle is not applied consistently and equitably. A two-tier system exists in which the average indirect cost recovery rate in 1985 was 58.9 points for private institutions and 42.0 points for public institutions. Public universities have little incentive to raise their cost recovery rates since recoveries would have to be remitted back to the state. Because private universities keep all funds recovered, they are more disposed to recover indirect costs up to the allowable limit.

The growing number of researchers and a shrinking pool of research dollars is intensifying competition for research financing. The federal government has responded by procuring research at the lowest cost and underfunding some projects, practices that ultimately threaten research quality. Moreover, talented scholars must spend time writing proposals instead of performing research.

The current system is unstable. If overhead rates rise, then even fewer funds will be available for direct research unless the total pool of dollars increases. In spite of strong incentives to control costs, deteriorating science facilities and equipment and increasing national concern about hazardous wastes are already pushing indirect cost rates up. The averaging principle of A-21 may still be the best approach, however. Many of America's best universities rely on it to maintain the excellence and scale of their research programs.

What should be done about research financing? Cognizant of the fact that the fruits of higher education's research programs provide a competitive edge for America in a changing economic world, Congress and the administration should fund scientific research adequately.

FUNDING INSTRUCTION
by Frank B. Campanella, *Executive Vice President,*
Boston College

The single largest expenditure for most institutions is faculty salaries and benefits. In all likelihood, inflation and faculty shortages in the next decade will spur further salary increases. Although most private institutions currently depend on tuition revenues to fund faculty salaries, some will turn to gift or endowment income to subsidize these costs because of pressure to limit tuition increases. Only the institutions with sufficient endowment or gift income will have this option, however.

As salary pressures mount, institutions will need better methods to measure and compare salary levels. At the institutional level, Campanella suggests developing a computer model to track average salaries by professorial rank and to analyze the impact of the forces that drive salaries (i.e., the number of faculty, salaries of new hires, promotions-in, promotions-out, and departures). He also suggests comparing percent changes in salaries by rank for continuing faculty across institutions using American Association of University Professors (AAUP) data and comparing continuing faculty salaries to changes in the Consumer Price Index. Cost and productivity studies are another important tool for tracking salary levels. Although these studies sometimes seem

5

threatening, it is possible for colleges and universities to perform them sensitively and with the cooperation of the department chair or manager. For example, Boston College's program was so well received that several departments requested productivity studies on their own initiative.

Financing communications and computer equipment is another challenging assignment for college and university administrators. It is likely that overall spending in these areas will continue to escalate as a result of rapid technological change and increased demand for maintenance and user support. As a financing vehicle, Boston College makes a cash transfer to the Plant Fund for the total amount of depreciation budgeted each year in the current fund. This cash is used to pay principal on long-term debt and to fund renewals and replacements. Any excess cash is invested in the Plant Fund for future financing of equipment purchases. To alleviate the institution's burden further, Campanella proposes increased corporate involvement and programs to encourage the voluntary purchase of personal computers on campus.

USING DEBT EFFECTIVELY
by Robert T. Forrester, *Partner,*
Coopers & Lybrand

America's colleges and universities floated an estimated $20 billion of tax-exempt debt from 1981 to 1986. This figure indicates that the effective use of debt is highly significant. Using three universities—Harvard, Brown, and Kentucky—as examples, Forrester proposes the following guidelines for using debt effectively:

- Seek the lowest overall cost of capital.
- Preserve debt capacity for periods of special need.
- Balance maturity risks between short- and long-term debt.
- Match sources of funding with particular projects.

- Make appropriate budgetary plans for repaying debt.
- Be aware of worldwide economic trends to minimize debt risks and costs.
- Consider and possibility of continuing regulatory threats to tax-exempt bonds.
- Separate the appropriation and financing decisions for capital projects.

Each of the three universities Forrester profiles has a different philosophy of debt. Brown is reluctant to borrow at all, while the University of Kentucky relies heavily on revenue debt. Harvard uses a combination of fund raising for major capital development or start-up costs, and debt for facilities renovation or where fees can be generated to repay the debt. Forrester concludes that each educational institution must ensure that its debt load is consistent with its financial and operating strategy.

TAXABLE FINANCING
by Arthur J. Kalita, *Managing Director,*
J. P. Morgan Securities

Since the Tax Reform Act of 1986, the tax-exempt market has become more volatile and taxable debt has emerged as a viable financing vehicle for higher education. Private institutions are now subject to a volume cap of $150 million of qualified 501 (c) 3 (tax-exempt) bonds outstanding per institution. Moreover, the Tax Reform Act set caps on student loan bonds, narrowed the definition of qualified 501 (c) 3 bonds, and established constraints on advance refunding and the financing of bond issue costs for tax-exempt debt.

Kalita asserts that these new limitations as well as some inherent advantages of taxable debt may make it more attractive to higher education than tax-exempt debt. In particular, colleges and universities can develop financing packages that are more responsive to their long-term financial needs, since a greater variety of taxable products is available. Although the interest

7

costs of taxable debt are higher, the cost of compliance with the new regulations and the inability to earn arbitrage profits on tax-exempt debt narrow the spread between the two financing vehicles. Kalita uses Cornell University, Texas A & M University, and the Virginia Education Loan Authority as examples of the effective use of taxable debt.

Colleges and universities should be aware of the domestic market (with foreign investor participation) and the international market (abroad) for taxable debt. Although these markets represent a sizable pool of funds, foreign investors are not yet very familiar with higher education bonds. Therefore, the near-term outlook for issuing college and university debt in foreign markets is not favorable, except for large single or pooled smaller issues of "name" institutions. Even domestically, foreign participation may mean higher direct costs to compensate for the novelty and relatively small issue size of the average institution's debt. The domestic private placement markets may offer the most flexible opportunities for higher education's taxable debt in the near term.

Kalita concludes that a critical task facing a college's financial officer will be selecting the best debt instrument to meet the institution's financial needs.

CREDIT ANALYSIS AND ENHANCEMENT
by Daniel Heimowitz, *Managing Director,*
Moody's Investor Services

Heimowitz maintains that higher education borrowers should know the basic principles of credit analysis and enhancement, especially since more colleges and universities are using the credit markets to finance capital projects.

If an institution's general credit is pledged, rating agencies consider its financial and strategic strengths as well as its capability to handle increased debt. Strong enrollment demand, a diverse income base, and sound overall financial performance are particularly important. For a public institution, rating agencies also consider the financial condition of the state or local government which supports the institution.

Institutions can improve the rating of a bond issue with outside credit support to enhance or substitute for the institution's own credit. The two most commonly used forms of credit substitution in higher education financing are bank letters-of-credit and bond insurance. If substitution is used, rating agencies evaluate the ability of the substituting entity to pay all principal and interest due the bondholders if the college or university defaults. If credit enhancement is used, a bank, or the borrower, bolsters a portion of the issue rather than assuming the entire risk. The credit enhancement takes the form of standby liquidity, securitization, or collateralization. For instance, colleges and universities may collateralize a bond issue with a portfolio of investments. Or they may use securitization by pooling assets, such as mortgages or receivables, to provide security for the debt issue.

MORTGAGE-BACKED STUDENT LOANS
by Douglas Wofford, *Research Associate,*
Forum for College Financing

As the cost of its product increases, higher education is considering greater involvement in financing tuition and other student costs. One relatively new option is mortgage-backed student loans, a vehicle that carries potential tax advantages for families. Under the Tax Reform Act of 1986, interest incurred on a residence-secured loan is deductible up to certain limitations.

The advantages of establishing an in-house mortgage-backed student loan program include the following:

- Provides a valuable service to families.
- Gives the institution a competitive advantage over others who do not offer such financing.
- May offer more effective service than private financial institutions can provide in terms of lower interest rates or more timely delivery to satisfy IRS requirements.

Before establishing a mortgage-backed student loan program, an institution might want to consider the public policy and administrative implications. Public policy considerations include such questions as the advisability of removing students from the debt agreement and the perception that higher education might be abusing the tax law for self-serving reasons. An institution also needs to consider its resources. A mortgage-backed student loan program requires legal advisors as well as administrative personnel who can become well versed in state statutes regarding second mortgages. Program administrators need a cooperative relationship with a title company (to perform title searches and mortgage recording), and either sufficient internal financial resources or a cooperative relationship with a bank (to cover up-front costs).

The University of Pennsylvania and the Massachusetts Education Loan Authority have implemented mortgage-backed student loan programs. Early indications suggest strong family interest in this loan option.

FINANCING HIGHER EDUCATION IN A GLOBAL ECONOMY
by Anthony D. Knerr, *Executive Vice President for Finance and Treasurer,*
Columbia University

Our nation is increasingly influenced by the international marketplace, and so are our colleges and universities. Knerr suggests that higher education will benefit by developing a more global orientation toward its economics and financing in response to the changing marketplace.

Over the next 10 to 20 years, higher education is likely to face the following:

• Rapid real escalation in expenses.
• Constrained financial resources.
• Greater complexity in management.

- The need for significant changes in the academic program and in institutional goals and assumptions.
- New levels of volatility in the economy and marketplace.

Knerr draws two major conclusions from the chapters in this book. First, higher education is in the process of evolving a more adequate conceptual model for its financing. Such a model will help clarify the implications of present trends for the future and permit improved insights into the interconnections among components of the underlying economic structure of colleges and universities.

Second, more than ever before public policy is influencing, and influenced by, higher education. In the absence of a coherent higher education policy, colleges and universities should take several steps:

- Explain more clearly the importance and value of higher education.
- Advocate a longer-term perspective at the institutional level.
- Become more aware of the vulnerabilities associated with changing public policies.
- Plan institutional responses to anticipated economic changes.

2

THE ECONOMY AND HIGHER EDUCATION

RICHARD E. ANDERSON

ACCORDING to some analysts the American economy is strong and the prospects for future growth are good. The most obvious and destructive problems, the budget and the trade deficits, have eased somewhat. The federal budget shortfall is still high by historical standards but it is not out of line with the budget deficits experienced by our major trading partners in the late 1970s and early 1980s. And, although the United States' widely publicized trade deficit is a major concern, the weak dollar has begun to energize our manufacturing sector.

Alarmists, on the other hand, point to the confluence of the trade and budget shortfalls and the long-term depressing effects of these deficits. They further observe that some of the reductions to the budget deficit are less significant than meet the eye and that a good part of the trade deficit is structural and will remain impervious to a weakened dollar. Finally, these pessimists point to the growing problem of unfunded pension liabilities and the general need to replace our infrastructure.

This chapter will consider the macroeconomic trends that shape our economy and the effects of those trends on higher education. Although the projections of the middle-of-the-road analysts will probably be more accurate than those of the extremists—things generally have a way of working out—the storm clouds are real and close enough that they bear serious attention. This chapter will, therefore, highlight the more pessimistic perspectives. If institutions are forewarned about these problems they will be in a better position to react should, or when, they need to.

___ THE ECONOMIC ENVIRONMENT

Productivity

If the United States is to enjoy financial prosperity, it must be productive. The more goods and services produced, the more we can consume. The generally accepted gauge of the strength of our economy is the level and changes in the Gross National Product (GNP). GNP is a measure, albeit an imperfect one, of the total goods and services we produce. Among its four major components are measures of (1) *goods and services consumed by households* and (2) *those provided by governments*. It also includes (3) *capital investment* in manufacturing facilities and equipment and in other private and public infrastructure like houses, roads, airports, and offices. All this fixed investment is necessary for the country and the economy to continue to grow. In addition, the GNP gauges (4) *net export* of goods and services. It is important to keep these four components in mind. An increase in the consumption of goods and services by households and governments translates into an immediately improved standard of living. Increases in the creation of public and private infrastructure creates capacity for future growth and future increases in our standard of living. The shipment of products and services abroad results in the claims on the wealth of other nations, claims which can be redeemed for future consumption or to build productive capacity.

Over the last three decades GNP has grown at about 3 percent per year above inflation but this growth rate has been trending downward since the 1970s. (See Figure 2-1.) There has been a spurt of growth in the last few years, but most experts discount these increases because they were induced by disproportionately high deficit spending. As a *Business Week* article observed, "growth under Reagan was stimulated by deficits . . . nothing more than Keynesianism on steroids."

An acknowledged problem with the GNP measure is that all goods and services are not counted. Economics texts are quick to point out that the work of housewives is excluded from the GNP (as is that of househusbands). Should a woman enter the workforce and hire domestic help, an event which is much more common today than in the past, the GNP would increase by the wages of both the wife and the domestic. If GNP is corrected for number of workers (see Figure 2-2.), the economic inertia of the last two decades is painfully obvious. Growth in GNP per worker has been practically non-existent since 1970. Again, only the deficit induced growth of the last few years breaks this trend.

Our lagging standard of living was a cause for concern in the late 1970s and helped propel Ronald Reagan into the White House and generate the supply-side experiment. Unfortunately, we didn't work any harder during the last eight years. What has changed has been our spending pattern. We're no more productive but we're spending (i.e., consuming) as if we were. The most obvious transgressor is the federal government as it runs up huge federal deficits unprecedented in a peacetime economy. Families are also borrowing more and saving less. Consumer debt, for example, has grown from 60 percent of GNP in 1980 to almost 80 percent in 1988. Similarly, savings in the United States declined from about 7 percent of GNP in the 1970s to an all-time low of about 3 percent in 1987. It has since rebounded to the 4 to 5 percent range but our national savings rate is among the lowest of the developed economies. Japan, a model for personal thrift, saves at a rate of about 12 to 16 percent. Savings in the Western European countries is in the 7 to 10 percent range.

We have also propped up our standard of living by importing more goods than we export. Trade surpluses soak up GNP,

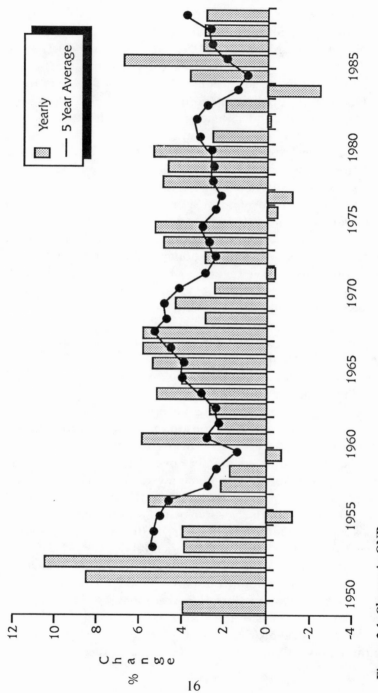

Figure 2-1. Change in GNP.

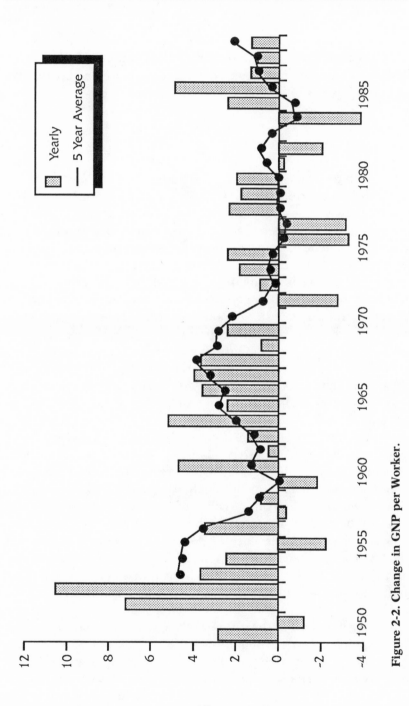

Figure 2-2. Change in GNP per Worker.

requiring families or governments to consume less. Trade deficits have the opposite result. Collectively, the United States has lived better by importing what we do not manufacture and borrowing or selling assets to finance this consumption.

The "Twin Deficits"

Both the trade and the federal budget deficits have received a good deal of attention in the popular press recently, concern that is very well deserved. Still, it is important to understand the magnitude of these deficits and the problems they create.

Some believe that the only proper status of the federal budget is balanced. This position is certainly too simple in a complex modern economy. It is expected that a government will spend more than it takes in during a war or other national emergency. Moreover, governments can reasonably use their spending authority to stimulate the economy during an economic slowdown. Ideally, budget deficits that spur the economy would be matched with budget surpluses created when the economy is strong. As Figure 2-3 shows, however, budget surpluses have been rare since 1960. Of greater concern is the uniformity and the magnitude of the budget deficits in recent years. Prior to 1980, the budget deficits, measured as a percent of GNP, swung from small positive balances to negative balances in the 2 to 3 percent range. (During many of these years we were financing the Vietnam conflict.) Only in 1975 did the deficit exceed 3 percent of GNP. Since 1982 the deficits have consistently exceeded 4 percent. In most of these years, the GNP has been growing so they cannot be characterized as "stimulative" deficits. The budget imbalance declined to just above 3 percent in 1987, but many economists are skeptical of this progress. They claim that some of the deficit reduction was achieved by selling assets and by the inclusion of social security surpluses in the deficit calculation, surpluses which we will need in the future as the elderly population grows.

Apologists for the deficits observe that Germany and Japan have run large negative imbalances in government spending for equally long periods of time. One difference is that, while their

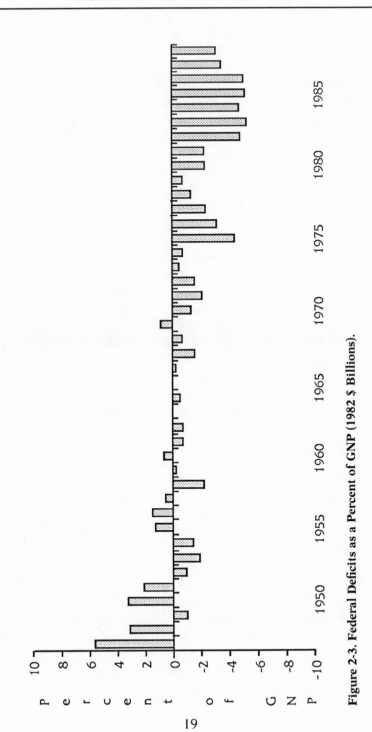

Figure 2-3. Federal Deficits as a Percent of GNP (1982 $ Billions).

deficits also occurred during periods of economic expansion, they were more than offset by large trade surpluses. Their deficits, in effect, helped to build productive capacity. The opposite is true in the United States in the 1980s. Figure 2-4 shows that since 1982 we have also had consistent, and extraordinarily high, trade deficits. In effect, our budget deficits have been financing consumption, not industrial buildup. During the last two decades American companies have shifted manufacturing capacity overseas. More and more U.S. production consists of assembling foreign-made components. This "hollowing" of our industry will take an equally long period to reverse and will slow any efforts to correct the trade imbalance.

Figure 2-5 offers a composite graph of our profligate behavior, displaying the sum of the two deficits as a percent of GNP. Until the late 1960s the trade and budget figures generally balanced each other. Under the economic strain of the Vietnam conflict, the total of the two deficits turned negative but was never more than 4 percent of GNP. Since 1983, both figures have been in the red and the sum is destructively high. The deficits have been financed partly by selling our assets but primarily by borrowing from foreigners. Consequently, real interest rates have been pushed to unusually high levels with wealth hemorrhaging from this country.

The exact effects of these large deficits are unknown, but one thing is certain; deficits of this magnitude will not continue into the indefinite future. Moreover, any delay in correcting the imbalances will exacerbate the problems. These problems can be classified as financial and structural.

Financial problems. The debt created by these deficits is the most obvious problem. In 1982 we were the world's largest creditor nation. Now we are the largest debtor nation, with net debt of approximately $700 billion. Moreover, it is impossible to turn these deficits around overnight. Most economists assert that *if* we sacrifice consumption and *if* we raise taxes, we can bring the deficits down to a manageable level. But to accomplish this in an orderly fashion without generating a recession, net debt will need to rise for some time, reaching a peak of perhaps a $1 trillion dollars. As a result interest, dividends, and rent paid to foreigners could exceed several percent of GNP in the 1990s.

Another financial problem created by these deficits is that real interest rates (interest adjusted for inflation) must be high enough to attract a sufficient number of purchasers of our debt. Historically, the rates paid on long-term Treasury debt have been about 1 percent above inflation. During most of the 1980s the real return to Treasury Bonds has been 4 to 5 percent above inflation. The recent record deficits and the need to fund them are one of the major reasons for these abnormally high interest costs—costs shared by all who wish to borrow, including colleges and universities. Unfortunately this problem can compound itself. If a country pays real interest at a rate which exceeds real growth, then the burden of debt grows ever larger.

A third financial consequence is that the value of the U.S. dollar is likely to remain low. Although the price at which foreign investors are willing to hold U.S. dollars is very complicated, the productivity and the expected productivity of the economy are major factors. To the extent that we drain our productive capacity with high debt to foreigners, the value of the dollar will be depressed. One consequence of a weak dollar is that domestic purchasing power will be further reduced. Foreign goods make up about 15 percent of the goods consumed in this country. If foreign goods rise 50 percent in price and consumption of foreign goods remains level (it will not but it has been surprisingly inelastic so far), families suffer a 7.5 percent decline in purchasing power.

Structural problems. During most of the 1980s, the U.S. economy grew at a satisfactory rate. The foundation of that growth, however, was consumption and not the creation of plant and equipment. Families and governments were spending at higher and higher levels and financing their purchases with debt. As a consequence the United States devoted fewer resources to plant and equipment. Entire industries developed offshore for which there is no domestic equivalent (e.g., consumer electronics). The lead in many other industries has shifted abroad (e.g., micro chips). In an effort to keep prices of domestically produced

21

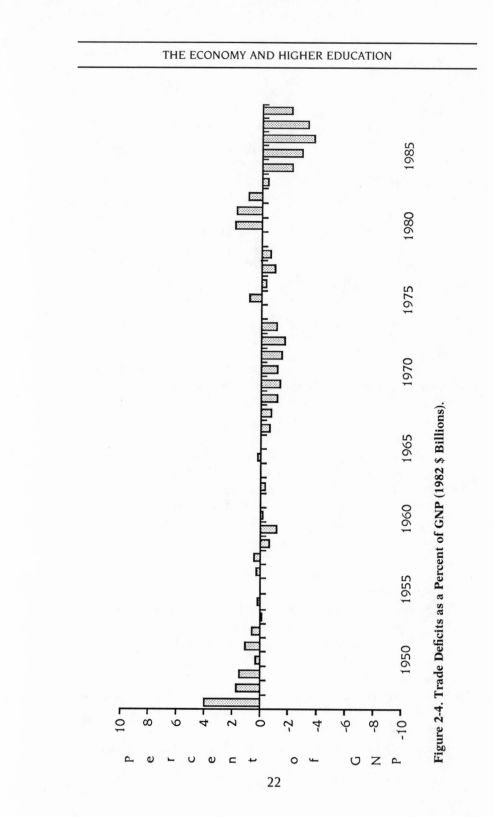

Figure 2-4. Trade Deficits as a Percent of GNP (1982 $ Billions).

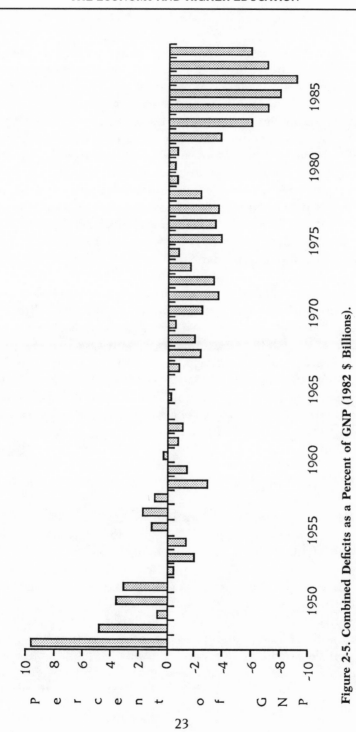

Figure 2-5. Combined Deficits as a Percent of GNP (1982 $ Billions).

goods as low as possible, many U.S. companies either moved production facilities abroad or imported major components for their products. A weaker dollar will tend to reverse this trend but it will take time to rebuild productive capacity.

It is important to note that most experts believe that a turnaround in trade is going to have to be led by manufacturing. It is a myth, according to these analysts, that we can prosper as a nation with a "service economy." One reason is that service that is exportable *and* that is not intricately tied to production is of too little consequence. Another reason is that there is no validity in the belief that this country can maintain a structural advantage in the production of services. The opposite, in fact, is likely to be true as many services in financial, legal, and other fields can be culture specific.

The weak dollar lowers the price to foreigners not only of U.S. manufactured goods but of U.S. manufacturing facilities. As treasury debt matures, some foreign creditors are deciding not to repurchase debt but to buy U.S. companies instead. Stephen Roach, a Solomon Bros. economist, estimates that foreigners already own 10 percent of U.S. manufacturing facilities and this percentage is growing very rapidly. The profits of these companies will flow into foreign bank accounts with further depressing effects on our standard of living.

Future Prospects

Best-case scenario. Projections about the strength of our economy vary widely but recall that growth in GNP per worker has been virtually level since the 1970s. Therefore, barring a resurgence in productivity that violently breaks this pattern, a best-case scenario is for modest growth and the avoidance of a severe economic downturn. But this best-case scenario is not necessarily a rosy one. The basic foundation for this projected growth is that a weak dollar will make American-made goods cheap on the world markets and revitalize our manufacturing sector—a structural change that is going to require significant investment in plant and equipment and, consequently, diminished domestic consumption. The plan also calls for our major trading partners to reduce their exports and absorb ours. If our trading partners do not consume more, the world marketplace will be glutted with goods and a worldwide recession (some whisper depression) could occur.

Furthermore, this plan calls for some improbable changes in the domestic economy. We still need to service the mountain of debt that has accumulated as we shift from consumption to investment. The prospects for an improved standard of living under this "optimistic" forecast, therefore, are not at all bright. Debt payments, exports, and investment in plant and equipment will consume a larger share of economic output. Meanwhile, the weak dollar, which is necessary to fuel manufactured exports, will make foreign imports more expensive. Former Commerce Secretary Peter Peterson estimates that to finance our debts and simultaneously to create the necessary productive capacity consumption must decline by about $165 per worker per year over the next decade. To put this in perspective, consumption per worker rose by about $200 per year in the 1970s—a period many considered austere. It is far from clear that we can generate the political will in this country to make these necessary adjustments.

Alternative to the best-case. If, as discussed above, each country tries to maintain its previous share of international commerce, a destructive trade war could result. The oversupply of goods will slow economic activity around the globe, bringing a worldwide recession. The domestic effect of our sharing in this recession would be a decline in personal income and tax revenues. The federal deficit would be likely to grow, making the debt payments even more onerous.

Other observers, focusing on third-world debt, proffer that even a mild cyclical recession could cause less developed countries to repudiate their debts, which are already extremely burdensome, as accounts from Latin America, and Africa make clear. Alfred Malabre, a senior editor of *The Wall Street Journal*, argues that the potential for an international debt crisis is very real and far more serious than in the 1930s. Reasons include the greater volume of debt, higher levels of international trade, and the commercial interdependence of economies. In addition, third-world nations are more politically independent today. Earlier in the century many of these nations were supported by a more stable colonial empire. The speed with which a crisis could develop is amplified by advances in transportation and communication. Finally, and perhaps most distressing, in earlier decades the leading economies (Britain, and then the United States) were relatively strong creditor nations. Today, in spite of its problems, the U.S. economy is still the most influential but is also the world's largest debtor. This debt greatly restricts policy options should a crisis occur. By 1992–93 the ratio of our foreign debt to exports could exceed 200 percent—a point at which many less developed economies have found debt too burdensome to service.

Another possible outcome, and not necessarily mutually exclusive of a recession, is double-digit inflation. Inflation diminishes the pain of debt as it allows the debtor to repay with a less valuable currency. The German inflation after World War I helped get that nation out from under war reparations but at a severe cost in productivity and social order. Inflation might be initiated in this country, for example, if the Federal Reserve expands the money supply in an effort to rescue failing financial institutions. (Immediately after the October 1987 stock market crash, the Fed promised "all the money necessary" to keep the stock market liquid.) Moreover, some observers believe that there is more bad debt in this country than is publicly acknowledged, an assertion that is bolstered by the farm credit problems, the savings and loan crisis, and veterans home loan program defaults.

Policy options are very slim, with one possible, and dangerous, exception. The social security system will be generating large surpluses in the coming years as the baby boomers reach peak earnings capacity. Although these surpluses are essential to finance the retirement of these same workers, the funds could provide some financial breathing room by reducing our dependence on foreign lenders. However, these funds also pose an almost irresistible temptation to politicians to postpone problems in the 1990s and, in the process, pass on calamity to the next century.

The policies of the last few decades, which encouraged consumption and discouraged savings, have created a situation with many problems and few policy options. Concern about economic well-being will dominate, even more than it does today, public and private decision making in the 1990s. These financial pressures will create problems and opportunities for colleges and universities with which they must be prepared to deal.

EFFECTS ON HIGHER EDUCATION

Perhaps in no time in recent economic memory has there been such focused concern on the U.S. economy. Headlines blare out: "America, Wake Up!," "A Troubled Economy," and "Are We a Second-Rate Economy?" Hyperbole, of course, helps to sell magazines and papers. There is, however, a growing consensus that we will have to get our national finances in order. The effects on higher education of this reordering of the economy will depend to a large extent upon whether higher education is seen as part of the problem or part of the solution. Put another way, does higher education represent consumption or investment? The glib response is that expenditures on higher education are an investment—an investment in human capital. This may be true but the United States "invests" more in higher education than any other country and proportionately more than our major trading partners (3 percent of GNP compared to 1.7 percent in Japan, .7 percent in Germany, and .8 percent in France). In spite of these relatively high educational expenditures, our economy has grown at a far slower rate than most others in the industrial world. Moreover, even if higher education is part of the "solution," that will not insulate it from demands for efficiency (i.e., doing the same for less) as family and public budgets are strained.

This section is divided into two parts. The first considers the effects of the protracted economic strains on colleges and universities. The second looks at likely roles for higher education in resolving America's competitiveness problems.

General Economic Strains

In the first part of this chapter is was argued that the coming decade is likely to be a financially spare one. As we repay our debts, build productive capacity, and export more goods, and as consumers pay a higher price for imports, the level of resources remaining to pay governmental and family expenses will be limited. This prospective austerity will affect all institutions including higher education.

Effects at the federal level. As a consequence of these economic necessities, the resources available for higher education from the federal government are not likely to grow, and may even shrink in real terms. All new program initiatives and the refinancing of existing programs will bump up squarely against the financial constraints caused by the deficit. Similarly, favorable tax treatment of higher education will be weighed against the government's need for new revenues without breaking President Bush's campaign promises to hold the line on taxes. This pressure is already evident as colleges and universities are finding it increasingly necessary to defend the tax-exempt status of endowments and parts of auxiliary enterprises. It is important, therefore, that higher education constituents work collectively to maintain the advantages they now have. More important, all institutions must avoid abuses of their tax status that could trigger either a legislative or regulatory assault.

New tax incentives to support higher education are extremely unlikely. One possible exception is that there may be an opportunity for tax advantaged savings that demonstrably increase family capital accumulation—but the savings would have to be clearly new and not displaced from other sources. The reason that special consideration might be given to savings incentives is that additional capital is needed to finance public and private infrastructure.

28

Inflation, should it reoccur, would put a special strain on the student aid budget that has been under attack for years. Between 1980–81 and 1987–88, federally supported student aid declined about 4 percent after adjusting for inflation. Virtually all of the cuts were sustained by the social security educational benefits and by veterans benefits. Pell grants, on the other hand, increased 17 percent. Part of the relief for general student aid was achieved because of lower nominal interest rates (real interest charges remain high through the time of this printing, but inflation dropped from 15 to 5 percent). Consequently the special allowance interest payment to lenders declined from 52 percent of Guaranteed Student Loan (GSL) costs in 1982 to 7 percent in 1987 (Source: College Board). Should double-digit inflation return, interest costs will rise dramatically and the entire federal student aid budget is likely to be distressed.

A recession, of course, would expand the deficit as revenues decline and transfer payments increase. This clearly exacerbates all problems discussed above. Until the federal budget is in closer balance, new broad-based assistance for higher education is unlikely. Specially focused programs that have the potential to provide direct improvement of American economic competitiveness will undoubtedly be enacted.

Effects at the state level.   The income and spending constraints of state governments will be similar to those at the federal level. Fortunately, states do not have as extensive a backlog of deficits as does the federal government. On the other hand, Steven Gold, director of fiscal studies for the National Conference of State Legislators, points out that state year-end general fund balances are precariously low. Since 1978, only 1983, a year at the tail end of a recession, showed lower year-end reserves. As a consequence, state budget options will be stretched by a laggard economy. A recession could cause a wave of state crises.

Although there are clear limits to states' abilities to finance education, including higher education, it has become a major policy issue. The reasons for increased state-level attention to education are complex and spring from a variety of public and private motivations, but clearly, desire to reinvigorate state econ-

29

omies is among the most prevalent causes. Linked to this is the concern that, although education is an important policy tool, the public is not getting its money's worth. Legislators and governors are demanding accountability in the form of evidence of educational achievement. If accountability is a manifestation of economic pressures, as I believe it is, the 1990s are unlikely to provide any relief to educational administrators. The opposite, in fact, should be expected. If economic strains grow—that is, if family incomes remain stagnant— the arguments may broaden from concerns about program and campus efficiency to basic questions about (1) sector roles (Should higher education be providing remedial instruction?); (2) access (How much higher education can we afford?); and (3) production technology (How important is tenure?). It is ominous that in Britain, a country whose economic weakness preceded ours, the protection afforded by faculty tenure has been significantly diminished.

Effects on institutions. Although financial stresses will affect public and independent institutions differentially, the general effects will be similar. Slow to no growth in family incomes will have a depressing effect on enrollments and, more specifically, on tuition income. A recession, however, could cause enrollments to spurt at public institutions. A weak dollar will reduce the cost of higher education to foreigners. Inflation will raise costs and high real interest rates. Finally, capital market volatility will generally increase the cost of financing and make investing more hazardous. In this environment independent colleges may be at special risk. Each of these eventualities will be considered briefly.

To paraphrase Mark Twain's famous telegram, past reports about the impending demise of private higher education have been greatly exaggerated. Is is possible, however, that these earlier concerns were well grounded and that only unanticipated intervention and events averted serious troubles. The rapid growth of federal student aid in the 1970s, for example, was just such a fortuitous intervention. Federal student aid adjusted for inflation doubled between 1970 and 1980. In addition, private higher education has undoubtedly benefited from the general,

30

even if ill-founded, economic confidence of the 1980s. Some set of parents, the exact proportion is unknown, may have been willing to extend themselves financially to pay for expensive private education because the economy seemed strong, the market value of their home provided a sense of wealth, or because the wife was able to find a job and maintain the family's life style. More generally, the 1980s were not a decade for American self-denial. If this attitude turns, and I am arguing that this change is inevitable, families will review expenditures, including those for higher education, much more carefully. Some real-estate markets have already begun to decline and a number of economists assert that a recession is overdue. Should economic problems become especially severe, the long heralded crisis in private higher education may arrive.

Perversely, a recession will magnify state financial problems but, as prior recessions have shown, an economic downturn is likely to result in increased demand for higher education as more young high school graduates cannot find a place in the workforce. This increased demand will, of course, be concentrated at the less expensive public institutions. In such an environment, public colleges may be asked to deliver more with less funding.

Any realistic projection of economic progress suggests that we will continue to need foreign capital for some time. As a consequence the dollar is predicted to stay depressed and real interest rates high. As noted earlier, the weak dollar will raise the cost of imports and reduce the purchasing power of domestic incomes. On the positive side, the sharp decline in the dollar should directly reduce the cost of American goods to foreigners. As it turns out, this generally hasn't occurred as manufacturers, wholesalers, shippers, and retailers all try to add on additional profit margins. But foreigners purchase higher education directly and these premiums are unlikely to appear—with the possible exception that state legislators may become restive about educating foreign competitors with public funds. Colleges that have strong programs for recruiting, assimilating, and educating foreign students should benefit immediately from the decline in the dollar.

Inflation, some analysts argue, is the only politically accept-able escape from our enormous public and private debt burdens. Double-digit inflation, *should it reoccur*, may affect institutions of higher education with special severity as it did in the 1970s. The generally accepted reasoning is that service industries, including higher education, are labor intensive. That is, their production process requires proportionately more labor than capital and, this conventional wisdom continues, it is inherently difficult to substitute capital (i.e., machines) for labor in service industries. Manufacturers, on the other hand, can tilt the production pro-cesses toward capital intensive machinery. Partially as a conse-quence of this shifting, the price of manufactured goods did not rise as rapidly as wages in the 1970s. Clearly there is some truth in this notion, but higher education would serve itself poorly by hiding behind such a shibboleth. Phone companies are in a ser-vice business, moreover one that is also engaged in information transmission, yet the real costs of telephone calls today are a fraction of what they were a few decades ago. This efficiency is a direct result of the effective use of technology. Higher education's apparent inability to use technology to reduce costs may have more to do with faculty values and the primacy of faculty gov-ernance than higher education's immutable production process. Institutions that can adapt technology successfully will be better suited to survive in an economy with limited growth and soaring prices. More generally, the coming decades are likely to require that colleges and universities devote some considerable attention to improving efficiency. Former Secretary of Education William Bennett has decried the rapid tuition increases of the 1980s. Those exhortations, while irritable in tone, continue to reflect a broadly based concern and were premonitory, not a divergent opinion.

An inflationary environment, coupled with this country's continuing need to attract foreign capital, will obviously push up interest rates. High real interest rates will encourage parental savings but will raise the cost of borrowing to states, institutions, and families. Once inflation has set in, parents and students will find debt a costly way to finance education. (During the process of inflation acceleration, debt burdens diminish.) Similarly, institutions that need to borrow to replace and renew plant and equipment will also find debt more burdensome.

In this prospective environment, capital markets are especially volatile, as recessions drag down nominal interest rates and inflation pushes them up. Colleges should be especially cautious when borrowing; interest rate caps on variable rate debt may be well worth the added cost. Volatile capital markets also demand special vigilance for the management of endowment, and a more conservative approach to investment strategies should be considered. The emerging standard for the 1990s is likely to be capital preservation.

Proactive Policies and Higher Education

William Baumol, a Princeton economist, observes that lagging productivity does not keep a nation from competing. Rather, it forces the country to compete in different ways—primarily through lower relative wages. In comparison to our major trading partners, wages in the United States have been declining for about two decades. Because of economic forces reviewed in this chapter, this trend may be irreversible for some time. In fact, wages may decline absolutely. Obviously, politicians and policy makers will not observe this trend passively. There will be positive, proactive responses. We have already suggested there will be increased scrutiny of public budgets. Efforts to improve the effectiveness of all public expenditures will be redoubled. Furthermore, budgets will be reorganized to target resources on areas that will have an immediate positive impact on our local, state, and national economies. All this is, of course, already occurring. The present analysis suggests that the problems will not pass quickly and that the coming environment is likely to be even more difficult.

High technology and science. At the postsecondary level, funding of science and technology will continue, as will government efforts to galvanize corporate and university partnerships.

So far most of the policy responses have been at the state level. Developmental corporations are being formed to smooth technology transfer from university laboratories to commercial production. In addition, states are encouraging, and sometimes financing, the development of research parks near universities. While anecdotal evidence suggests that these efforts can be successful, systematic reviews are just getting underway.

The federal government, relying primarily on macroeconomic policy, has lagged behind the states in developing these more micro activities. One notable exception is Sematech, a federally funded project at the University of Texas at Austin. This venture will bring together researchers from the university and from the leading semiconductor producers in the United States. The goal of Sematech is to re-establish our lead in the production of state-of-the-art semiconductor chips. If Sematech is successful, and if the state ventures prove successful, more funds and energy will follow.

These initiatives are, of course, welcome. They probably cannot be halted. But higher education should be cautious. As Thomas Jefferson warned the nation against "entangling alliances," these relationships are potentially constraining, even repressive. The University of Rochester stumbled when it briefly caved in to pressure from its benefactor, Eastman Kodak, and withdrew the acceptance of an applicant employed by Fuji Corporation. In this era of trade vulnerability, it is not difficult to imagine restrictions on foreign graduate students working in labs funded with federal money. Moreover, there will be a multitude of lively contests in the general arena of intellectual property rights as public funding authorities, corporations, universities, and faculty vie with one another for a "fair share" of generated gains.

Mid-level technology and industrial extension. Scientific progress is obviously important to mankind in many ways, including economically. But national success at the scientific frontier does not necessarily translate into national economic success. High technology breakthroughs are expensive to achieve

34

and difficult, as well as undesirable, to protect with patents. The success of America's trading partners was not built on expanding the frontiers of science but on adapting science to products and to the production processes.

As we maintain our strength in basic science we must also ensure that technological innovations find their way into the industrial process—this, of course, is the technology transfer issue that has stimulated "incubator" programs, university-business cooperation, and science parks. There is, however, a more prosaic technology transfer that must occur: the transfer of mid-range technology to the design, manufacture, and distribution of goods. Certainly this is happening but not on the necessary scale. Moreover, too much of the innovation is limited to large, well-capitalized corporations within certain sectors. Higher education can play an important role in bringing technological innovations to companies of all sizes and in all sectors of manufacturing.

Industrial extension, an analog to agricultural extension, has already been suggested and is being attempted at some large public universities. The idea needs to be further refined and expanded. For example, university-based research and development parks are typically built on high technology cores; the concept is that a concentration of scientists will form a synergy resulting in new ideas and new products. Their focus is on science and scientific products. Generally, covenants for these parks significantly restrict the type and amount of manufacturing in which tenants may engage.

As an alternative to science parks, states could create high technology production parks that invite companies involved in certain types of production to become tenants. The parks could be built near a university and some part of the lease payments would support process development laboratories. It is conceivable that the state might match these funds. In addition to the university's role, community colleges could be enlisted to train students in the repair and service of related equipment.

Some years ago I was employed as a production engineer with General Electric. One plant at which I worked was devel-

35

oping a new process for manufacturing industrial capacitors. The developmental work was being done in a remote part of the facility, with those engineers being both socially and physically isolated. For most of us, our work day centered on production schedules, labor relations, cost containment, and similar concerns. The development engineers had no colleagues. A production park that had, for example, a commitment to metal shaping and joining could help to create the same synergy in production that we are trying to build in science. This type of corporate-higher education partnership does not have the glamor of recombinant genetic research or of super-conductivity, but it may have more immediate economic impact. Moreover, it probably provides a better fit with regional universities and certainly with area community colleges.

As higher education moves closer to industry there are many academic and economic problems to be resolved, ranging from faculty compensation to site selection to efficient public subsidies. We must find answers to these problems if we are going to involve higher education effectively in national and local economic resurgence.

Foreign studies and modern languages. One area of the liberal arts that is likely to prosper in the emerging global economy will be foreign studies and modern languages. For decades this country has charted its own scientific and economic course and the rest of the world has followed. As our technological and commercial hegemony wanes, traffic on these streets will increasingly flow in two directions. A number of the trade problems with Japan, for example, are attributed to cultural misunderstandings. There will be more demand for people who can communicate with and understand the cultures of our global partners—not just the major trading nations but lesser developed countries also where we will compete to place manufacturing facilities. Similarly, we can no longer assume that all major technological innovations will be immediately published in English, so demand for translators is likely to grow. Institutions that maintain effective foreign studies and language programs should benefit.

Need for Balance

In this scenario of increasing attention to economic success, the tensions between the liberal arts and the science's and other more directly commercial fields of study can only increase. As the goals of families and legislators bend even more toward preserving and improving their personal and public economies, college administrators and trustees will need to be watchful that an appropriate equilibrium is maintained. In addition, they must avoid short-term answers to long-term problems. Broadly educated, self-reflective, articulate graduates will be more valuable to the nation, economically and otherwise, than narrowly trained technicians.

Related to the question of balance of institutional mission is the danger that colleges and universities will promise more than they can truly deliver. In the 1960s and 1970s higher education was enlisted in the war on poverty. In fact, we were more than passive conscripts; we welcomed public funds and became active partners in promising an excellent education and upward socioeconomic mobility to all who would spend four years. Subsequently we found public, especially federal, support to be inherently unstable, bringing attendant financial problems to our institutions. Real troubles, however, resulted from our inability to deliver on our promises. Simply stated, we failed to deliver upward socioeconomic mobility on the scale promised, and enrollments and public support waned. In retrospect the failure was inevitable. There wasn't enough room in the upper socioeconomic strata for the 60 percent of the age cohort who enrolled in our institutions.

The parallel concern today is that we may reorient our institutions to deliver economic growth that will halt the Japanese juggernaut. Having restructured our institutions, we could find that the ascendance of our trading partners is not easily reversed or that we were fighting to wrong battle. Public policy, and funding, may turn elsewhere and leave colleges with the fixed costs of laboratories and business schools and a faculty too narrowly trained in the hard sciences and commerce.

37

═ SUMMARY

The real gross national product grew at an impressive 3.8 percent in 1988 and, as of this writing, there are few signs of the long-expected recession. Unemployment is still low and consumer spending remains strong. But current successes (or immediate problems) do not eliminate the pressing need to reduce the federal deficit, raise exports, and increase savings so that we can rebuild public and private infrastructure. The longer we wait, the more disruptive the reckoning.

Gross national product has four components: family consumption, government spending, capital investment, and net export of goods and services. As net exports rise, other components of the GNP must decline proportionately. To raise exports the United States must increase investment in plant and equipment, further diminishing the share going to family consumption and government spending. Moreover, much of government spending is unavoidable, ballooning debt payments being one inevitable expense. Unless this country's productivity is accelerated beyond its current lackluster standard, the prospects for a significantly improved standard of living are not bright.

The dependence of the United States on foreign capital will continue pushing interest rates upward and depressing the dollar. (A lower dollar will further diminish U.S. living standards.) We will, or course, learn to live within our means. But unless the transition to a more provident economy is coordinated with an increase in consumption by our trading partners, a major recession could occur. (Many economists argue that a cyclical recession is already overdue.) A recession, regardless of its cause, would exacerbate public and private budgetary problems. In addition, the threat of inflation remains as policy makers seek a politically acceptable escape from our debt problems.

Disruptions in capital markets will make debt financing, fund raising, and investment management more difficult. Although institutions will still try to achieve growth, attention to capital preservation will be important. High interest rates could severely disrupt Washington-based student aid as high GSL interest payments drain away federal support.

Voters will resist increased public spending as they try to minimize taxes and maintain personal living standards. Public funding for higher education will be most easily achieved when there are direct and measurable benefits—particularly economic ones. Similarly, personal incomes will be strained and family expenditures on higher education more closely examined. Moreover, our anemic savings rate and the growing number of two-income families are worrisome trends for private higher education. The typical family in the coming decade will have neither banked sufficient cash nor have a reserve worker (i.e., an educated housewife) for paying pricey tuition bills. Quality institutions will survive but glossy brochures and a "distinguished past" will be insufficient evidence of value. The current public and private call for productivity and accountability from colleges and universities could be only a murmur compared to the prospective clamor of the next decade.

An earlier version of this chapter appeared in 1988 as an edition of *Capital Ideas*, published by the Forum for College Financing.

3

FINANCING
RESEARCH

WILLIAM F. MASSY

SCIENTIFIC research has long been viewed as necessary for the continued improvement of man's condition, and, from a national economic perspective, the competitive position of the United States in the global economy. Most of the basic research in this country, and much applied research, is performed at universities. The American model combining graduate education and research is the envy of the world. Efficient support of university-based research and associated graduate training programs is one of the few policy options available to the United States as we struggle to maintain a competitive economy.

Despite the great success and perceived importance of university research, the mechanisms by which it is financed are under great stress. Ironically, federal budget shortfalls that stem, in part, from our loss of world economic leadership are a major cause for the pressure on research financing. In this environment it is especially important that Congress and the administration take a long-term view concerning the funding of scientific research and maintenance of research capacity.

Stress on the current system of financing university research is manifested in two ways. First there is disagreement about how the indirect costs of the research should be funded; second the process by which research projects are awarded has been politicized and fragmented. In this environment the potential is very great for damage to universities and their ability to maintain our national leadership in research and graduate education.

The indirect cost problem is caused by a combination of economic and systemic factors. ("Indirect cost" consists of overhead items such as general and administrative expense, and building depreciation, operations, and maintenance.) The effects are compounded by the failure of many principals in the research process to understand overhead and its relation to direct costs, university economics in general, and even their own long-term self-interest.

Politicization and fragmentation of the research award process results from an oversupply of expert researchers relative to available funding.[1] For nearly four decades now, university graduate programs have been producing large numbers of doctoral students trained in advanced research. Such training is important in its own right, but it also is produced jointly with research. Indeed, the combination of research and graduate training is widely held to be responsible for the universities' (and the country's) comparative advantage in research.

Unfortunately, the natural rate of production of doctorates, based on historical research funding, seems to be incompatible with present and planned future levels of research funding. The competition among an ever-larger cadre of researchers for an increasingly inadequate (from their standpoint) supply of funds is the driving force behind the politicization and fragmentation of the awards process.

OMB CIRCULAR A-21: LOGICAL, BUT NOT WITHOUT PROBLEMS

Indirect costs are defined and allocated to sponsored research according to guidelines of office of Management and Bud-

1. This is not to say that there is an oversupply relative to the need for the fruits of research.

get (OMB) Circular A-21. Originally developed during the 1950s as a joint effort of university administrators and the federal government, A-21 has become the Bible of university cost analysis. The guidelines are entirely logical. They are based on generally accepted accounting principles, and many refinements have been made over the years. A-21 also allows flexibility in the application of costing principles, which is valued because it minimizes the degree of intrusion of accounting upon academic program, organization, and culture. But despite this logic and flexibility, or perhaps because of them, A-21 has not settled the question of how the indirect costs of research should be financed.

Although no changes in A-21 are pending, observers of the indirect cost scene believe that pressures for additional revision are building in OMB and funding agencies such as the National Institute of Health (NIH), and possibly in Congress as well. These pressures led the Association of American Universities (AAU) to create a special committee in 1987 on indirect cost recovery, chaired by Provost Niel Pings of the University of Southern California. The committee examined data and met with faculty, university administrators, and government administrators. It reviewed the issues and made recommendations for dealing with them.[2]

It would be hard to invent a research financing system that is more unstable and vulnerable to attack in today's circumstances than the one we have now. Alas, no more effective system has yet been found.

Average, Not Marginal Cost

A-21 calls for average costing in an area that traditionally was funded on a marginal cost basis. Before the growth of government-sponsored university research after World War II, most research sponsorship came via foundation grants or gifts from individuals. This support was viewed by faculty, their institutions, and providers alike as supplementing the university's

2. The author was a member of this committee. The report can be obtained from the AAU in Washington, D.C.

regular programs. The infrastructure needed to service these modest activities was already in place, so it was natural for sponsors to pay only the direct cost of the work. Even the marginal indirect costs (such as extra accounting transactions) induced by foundation grants could be ignored because of the low level of activity.

The fact that growth in federal research volume soon overwhelmed the universities' administrative apparatuses and physical plant induced the government to start paying a "fair share" of the infrastructure costs. This led to the development of A-21, which was based on the "averaging principle": If sponsored research is X percent of total institutional activity, then the same percentage of infrastructure expense should be covered by research sponsors. Averaging is intended to approximate the flow benefits from infrastructure to outputs such as instruction and research. An approximation is needed, of course, because usually it is not possible to measure these flows directly.

The averaging principle is logical and conceptually simple, but not as easy to understand as the older process of computing payment of only the direct cost of research. Direct cost was confused with marginal cost, and many faculty members still believe in the marginal costing tradition. Most private foundations continue to view their activities as supplementary, so they pay only modest overhead—perhaps intended to cover the short-run marginal indirect cost of the work, but almost surely falling short of long-run marginal cost. Universities seldom try to collect overhead on activities funded as gifts, which also helps keep the marginal costing tradition alive.

Averaging Rules Are Complex, Arcane

Computing average cost sounds easy, but defining averages that reasonably approximate flows of benefits in complex organizations like universities is actually an extremely difficult task. "Weighting" is a major problem, for instance: Does a dollar of direct expense or a square foot of space devoted to research make the same demands on administration and operations and maintenance as a similar increment of instructional activity? Pages of arcane definitions and rules have been developed to deal with such questions. The problem is exacerbated by interuniversity differences in organization structures and accounting systems. Still more definitions and guidelines are needed to accommodate these differences to everyone's satisfaction.

The Process Is Closed, Often Adversarial

Complex rules beget the need for professionals to interpret them and, in the case of A-21, perform the needed costing studies, which are themselves subject to government audit. Highly trained and dedicated people from universities and government confront one another in the audit process and across the negotiating table. All too often, territoriality becomes a dominant issue, or positions dictated by self-interest are rationalized as adherence to accounting principles. It is very difficult for lay people in government or universities to understand the essentials of the negotiations, or to appreciate fully the critical issues. The process looks like a "black box" and is subject to misinterpretation and mistrust. This has undermined the sense of partnership that characterized the early years of university research support by federal agencies.

The influence on relationships between university administrators and faculty principal investigators is divisive as well. Indirect cost rates and collections have become "we/they" propositions rather than facets of a common research effort to fund research costs. The fact that A-21 was developed without significant input by practicing faculty or scientific societies does not help the situation.

Three Sets of Values Are Involved

Setting indirect cost rates is a three-party negotiation on many campuses—the government, the university administration, and its faculty. The faculty are expected to obtain their own research support, usually with minimal direct help from their institution.[3] Hence, principal investigators view grant and contract funds as *their* money, some of which the institution siphons off for purposes not demonstrably related to the project in question. High indirect cost rates invariably raise the concern of noncompetitiveness in funds acquisition. Therefore, the dynamics of the three-party negotiation are complex and potentially unstable.

Despite the prefix in the word "university" implying agreement, resource decisions in academe require balancing heterogeneous and often mutually inconsistent values. Science faculty have different objectives than do humanities faculty, for instance, so the idea that overhead payments may somehow find their way to the English department does not relieve criticism from all sides. Indeed, suspicion about cross-subsidies can be very divisive, especially when the alleged recipients of the subsidy seem ungrateful and even envious of the science faculty's extra support and perquisites.

Nor do appeals about institution-wide need for funds elicit much support for payment of overhead. The perceived linkage between incremental dollars and the general well-being is too tenuous.[4] Faculty often care more about their own research, graduate students, department, and "invisible college" (academic field) than about the university as such. Although support for overhead recovery sometimes can be marshaled in times of fiscal crisis, it is hard to find in "normal" times.

The three-party negotiation is further complicated by the fact that government program officers and advisory panel members usually were once faculty members. Their negative perceptions about indirect costs are induced by, and reinforce, the feelings of the practicing faculty. Principal investigators are often pressured by program officers to obtain overhead waivers, and they willingly (sometimes enthusiastically) pass this pressure along to university administrators.

3. To be fair, there is little opportunity for such help as long as awards are based on scientific peer review.
4. Such arguments are more likely to be met with demands that administrative costs be cut.

The Free-Rider Problem

Overhead charges, like taxes, are subject to the free-rider problem. The use of benefits funded by overhead does not depend materially on one's own overhead payments. There is a fallacy of composition. The indirect cost recovery on a single project is not that critical, but aggregate recovery is very significant. What is best for one principal investigator (for example, waiver of overhead) would be disastrous if pursued successfully on an institution-wide basis.

A-21, for all its logic, cannot mitigate the free-rider problem. Willing compliance with a tax requires that the common benefits be well defined and widely supported, that the tax calculation be understood and accepted, and that enforcement of the tax be perceived as consistent and equitable. The preceding argument demonstrates that A-21 falls short on the first two criteria. Let us now turn to the questions of consistency and equity.

___ THE TWO-TIERED MARKET

Any assertion that the averaging principle of A-21 is consistently and equitably applied across the population of research universities is undermined by empirical data on indirect cost rates. Data from the U.S. Department of Health and Human Services covering the 118 institutions of which they are cognizant show that, for 1985, indirect cost rates ranged form 30 to 99 points, with a mean of 45 points.[5] It is difficult to believe that differences in scale and mix of operations, characteristics of physical plant, regional economic differences, and administrative efficiency could produce so much variation in overhead rates. Therefore, it appears that the averaging principle applies itself differently in different situations.

5. One percent of schools was below 30.6 points and 1 percent was above 99 points. The 5th and 95th percentiles were 35.1 and 75.0 points, and the 25th and 75th percentiles were 41.0 and 57.7 points. Source: U.S. Department of Health and Human Services, with calculations by Coopers & Lybrand.

47

Public or private status of an institution is an important indicator of its indirect cost rate. In the above mentioned study, the average rate for private institutions was 58.9 points and that for publics was only 42.0 points. This is consistent with Stanford's survey of 12 private and 9 public universities, where the average for 1986 was 62.6 points for the privates and 43.5 points for the publics.

Perceptions about consistency and equity in A-21 are tainted by the practice of distributing a portion of indirect cost recovery back to faculty as direct research support. This practice is not uncommon, especially among public universities, but the incidence, amount, and manner of distribution vary greatly. The distributions are extraordinarily popular, since they can be used for support of graduate students between grants, foreign travel, and other purposes that are difficult or impossible to fund conventionally. But it is hard to reconcile such allocations with the publicly asserted reasons for collecting overhead in the first place—the recovery of infrastructure expense. How, some people ask, can some institutions maintain a low overhead rate and yet make overhead money available to help principal investigators pay direct research costs? Unfortunately, the answer often is that the application of the indirect cost system is illogical and inequitable.

The effect of public universities' lower indirect cost rates and their greater tendency to return overhead to principal investigators is to produce a two-tiered pricing system for research, similar to the two-tiered system of tuition rates. Private universities compete constructively with their public counterparts in ways that, they hope, can make up for the tuition differential. The same is true in the research arena. Why are indirect cost rates, like tuition rates, lower in the public sector than the private sector? A growing body of evidence indicates that many public institutions have little incentive to raise their rates so that recovery makes a substantial contribution to fixed costs. Such recovery would have to be remitted to the state, either directly or in subsequent negotiation in the following years.[6] It appears that

6. The state, naturally enough, views itself as funding the fixed costs already.

such institutions are content to recover an approximation of the marginal indirect costs of sponsored research. Private institutions keep all the money they recover and so have every incentive to maximize contribution to fixed costs under the averaging principle.

This proposition raises two important questions

- Is it possible, under A-21, to negotiate indirect cost rates that do not include the proportional contributions to fixed costs called for under A-21?

    The answer is an unequivocal yes. Decisions about the weightings mentioned earlier could produce this result. Furthermore, NIH has been negotiating rates below those calculated by the institution, and there is no reason why these rates could not be at marginal indirect cost or even below.[7]

- Can the marginal indirect costs of research be quantified to the point where policy formulas could be based upon them?

    The answer to this question is an unequivocal no. Part of the problem stems from the variety of definitions available for marginal indirect costs (for example, long- or short-run marginal costs), and part from the difficulty of measurement. Although marginal indirect costs are known to be significant, neither the government nor universities can estimate them with enough precision to use them as a basis for policy making.

Understanding the economic forces that shape the two-tiered overhead pricing system is important both for its own sake and for assessing the integrity of the overall system. We must face the question of whether the observed range of overhead rates can possibly represent a consistent application of the averaging principle.

7. It is reported that in some cases NIH refuses to negotiate rates by indirect cost pool component, but instead focuses only on the overall rate. It is difficult to reconcile this approach with careful adherence to the averaging principle.

___ A MONOPSONIST UNDER PRESSURE

The federal government is a monopsonist of university research. Individual federal agencies, such as NIH, also have monopsonistic power in their areas of specialization. That is, the federal government and its agencies dominate the supply of research and can extract unjustified economic concessions from sellers by playing off one against the others. Research funding by industry, foundations, and private individuals is not a feasible alternative to federal support.

Until recently, the "market power" of the federal research buyer was constrained by:

- a sense of partnership between government agencies and the leading universities, which included long-run research capacity building.
- adherence to the principle of full recovery of average costs as calculated under A-21.

These positions were mutually reinforcing, and they were maintained by a combination of government self-interest and political forces.

Two things have changed as of the late 1980s. First, there is the oversupply of trained researchers noted earlier. The number of faculty openings at the leading universities is smaller than the doctoral output of these same institutions, so there is underemployment of trained individuals and a growing desire of "have not" institutions that have employed these well-qualified researchers to become "haves" with respect to federal funding. Second, the desire to balance the federal budget limits the available research funding despite the strong need for research results. The collision of these forces has put great pressure on the research partnership and the principle of full average cost recovery.

This pressure manifests itself in efforts by federal agencies to procure research at the lowest available cost, possibly from sources with low negotiated overhead rates or high rates of institutional cost sharing. Emerging institutions, which have not yet begun to rely on the contribution of sponsored research to fixed infrastructure expense, are often glad to discount proposals to marginal cost or even below. Political intervention on behalf of the have-nots is another competitive weapon and, at times, there are attacks on the scientific merit review itself.[8]

Efforts by federal agencies to spread the available money around, even at the expense of underfunding individual projects, have become common. The result is fragmentation of research effort, with principal investigators submitting more proposals of smaller average size in order to maintain their programs. A rising overhead rate puts the investigator in a double bind, where the resources remaining for direct deployment may no longer be sufficient to support the work of even one graduate student. No wonder the frustration of many principal investigators is reaching the boiling point.

Is the heightened competition good or is it destructive, perhaps to the point where the health of the U.S. science industry is in jeopardy? There may be real cause for concern—not about the competition itself, but about the forms it is taking.

The idea that scarce resources for scientific research should be allocated on the basis of any criterion other than the most rigorously demonstrated scientific merit in relationship to cost is shortsighted. Our country depends so much on the results of science that political interference with resource allocation efficiency should not be tolerated.

One should remember that although indirect cost rates range from 35 to 90 percent, the actual costs of individual projects vary much more narrowly. According to a Cornell University study, the total cost of a hypothetical "benchmark" research project ranged from \$260,000 to \$347,000 over a sample of 113 institutions.[9] This is a factor of only 1.33:1, much lower than the

---

8. Critics argue that the system is self-perpetuating in that it is staffed by well-established faculty at the leading universities.

9. James J. Zuiches and Rebecca Vallely, "Accounting for the Full Costs of Research: A Study of Indirect Costs," Office of the Vice President for Research and Advanced Studies, Cornell University (final prepublication draft, September 27, 1987, p. 48). The sample of 113 institutions was drawn from the 118 institutions of the NIH database.

factor of almost 7:1 for raw indirect cost rates. The difference stems from variations in accounting practices and policies concerning what must be charged directly to a project rather than being supplied as part of the overhead.

Differences in the scientific quality of proposals can be expected to dwarf cost variations of 1.33:1. Surely, concentration on small cost variations to the detriment of quality differences would be shortsighted. Judging relative cost on the basis of raw indirect cost rates is not justified.

Fragmentation reduces the efficiency of the research process itself, because it requires talented investigators to spend a disproportionate amount of time writing proposals and handling paperwork. Moreover, the effect of "sharing the wealth" is to put more money in the hands of investigators who might not have passed peer-group review had grants been fewer and fully funded. If one believes in the efficacy of scientific peer review, it follows that using a fixed budget to accommodate ever larger numbers of would-be investigators is in conflict with the goal of resource allocation efficiency.

Another problem with the current competitive intensity in regard to research funding is that, increasingly, the government is allocating resources according to procurement rather than investment criteria. But science cannot be "procured" like so much hardware or personal services. World-class science demands an investment point of view, where "patient money" seeks and nurtures the greatest possible excellence. That was the view of the Department of Defense, beginning in the 1950s, and the National Science Foundation and National Institutes of Health in the later years of the government-university research partnership. Now, unfortunately, that partnership is being sorely tested.

⎯ MOVEMENT IS LIKELY,
⎯ BUT WHICH WAY?

Our present system of funding university research is unstable. Significant change seems possible, even likely, but the direction of change is not clear. Decisions made during the next five years will affect American scientific research for decades.

Why is the system unstable? Although everything mentioned above contributes to this instability and affects the direction of movement, the potential for further increases in overhead rates will probably be the factor that triggers change.

State government may press more aggressively for full average cost recovery by public universities. States have an incentive, especially if they run into financial difficulties as the federal government reduces its funding of state programs. Although federal auditors will surely resist such increases, they cannot prevent them permanently unless Circular A-21 is altered.

The effect of such actions on the federal research budget could be dramatic, as shown by the following "back of the envelope" calculation.

> Federal research and development (R&D) obligations to colleges and universities were about $6.75 billion in 1985. The average indirect cost rate for the 118 institutions in the NIH database was 42 percent of modified total direct cost (MTDC). The Cornell study mentioned above found that MTDC was about two-thirds total direct costs.[10] Projecting these figures to all universities implies indirect cost payments of about $1.5 billion and direct charges of $5.25 billion. If all the public institutions went to full average cost recovery, their mean rate might approximate that for private institutions (about 59 percent), which then would become the overall mean. This would imply indirect costs of $1.9 billion and direct costs of $4.85 billion, assuming no change in total obligations. This is a shift of $400 million from direct to indirect costs.

The deplorable state of university science facilities and equipment is the second force pushing up indirect cost rates. Unless new federal facilities programs are authorized and funded, universities will have to borrow heavily and allocate a large proportion of the interest payments to sponsored research.[11] A third force affecting indirect cost rates is the in-

10. Ibid., p. 17.
11. Depreciation and use charges will also increase sharply.

creasing national concern about animal care, hazardous materials, and similar matters. Indirect cost will increase as universities struggle to alleviate these concerns. It is not difficult to envision scenarios where $100 million or more is shifted from direct to indirect cost.

The proportion of Public Health Service outlays to universities being charged to indirect costs increased by 12 percent between 1981 and 1985.[12] Other things being equal, the effect of shifting another $500 million in 1985 dollars from the direct to indirect category would have been a 25 percent increase on top of the 12 percent increase already incurred.[13] Such an increase would intensify efforts to "stop the runaway escalation of indirect costs" by amending A-21.

If history is any guide, these efforts would involve proposals to cap certain components of the overhead rate on the theory that:

- The measurements called for in A-21 are too difficult to verify.
- Universities have insufficient incentives to control expenses when average costs are recovered from research sponsors.
- It is not appropriate for the government to pay the full average cost of research.

A fixed allowance has already been adopted for departmental administration expense. The university community concurred because measuring departmental administration required faculty effort reporting—a notoriously obstructive and

12. The fraction was 0.138 in 1985, up from 0.284 in 1981—a 12 percent increase. These figures are weighted averages, in contrast to the unweighted averages of indirect cost rates used in the text above. The rate for universities is less than that for hospitals (20.7 percent), state and local governments (17.6 percent), and other nonprofit organizations (17.6 percent). Commercial entities increased more slowly (2.6 percent), but from a larger base (0.455 in 1981). Source: Public Health Service memorandum dated March 4, 1987.

13. The public universities would doubtless move items now charged as direct into the indirect pools, thus mitigating the actual effect, but 25 percent is what would show up in the NIH statistics.

unreliable process.[14] However, the measurement problem did not arise in allocating departmental administration between teaching and research. It arose in estimating the size of the overall pool. Departmental administration is the only indirect cost pool for which total expenditure is not precisely defined by the university's accounting system.

What about incentives to control indirect costs? Those of us who grapple with budget problems will testify that the incentives to control costs, especially administrative and support costs, are strong. Trustees and faculty committees oversee budget decisions, and we feel acutely the resistance to price increases of tuition and indirect cost payers.

The most convincing evidence for cost control is that, for most overhead components, university "copayments" run in the range of 50 to 75 percent under full average costing. Every dollar of incremental expense requires an outlay of 50 to 75 cents from university funds, with no possibility of recoupment; research sponsors pay the rest. In contrast, most knowledgeable observers of the healthcare industry agree that a 25 percent copayment is sufficient for cost control.

This returns us to the original question: Why is it appropriate for government to pay average, not marginal, costs? There are two strong reasons why reimbursement policy should continue to be based on full average cost recovery.

The first reason is that the alternative—marginal cost—is nearly impossible to calculate in a consistent and equitable way. No reliable method has been devised for estimating marginal indirect costs, and none is on the horizon. A monopsonist, even the government, cannot be trusted to bargain about price in the absence of a regulatory policy formula that can be consistently and equitably applied.

The second reason for retaining full average cost recovery is that many of America's best universities depend on it to maintain the excellence and scale of their research programs. Private institutions must fund themselves from tuition and sponsored research receipts, supplemented by endowment payout and

14. Also, the amount of money at stake for most institutions was small.

expendable gifts. The latter are already being utilized to the limits of prudence, so any decline in per-unit research receipts would have to be offset by higher tuition or reduced program quality.

My rough calculation of the effect of reducing the overhead recovery of private institutions down to the public university average is that private *tuition would rise by as much as one-third*, all else being equal. The alternative would be to reduce quality of both teaching and research. Quality reduction would, in turn, raise serious questions about the efficacy of paying today's tuition, given the public university alternative.

In other words, "leveling down" the two-tiered pricing system for research would place the private sector in an impossible position with respect to the two-tiered pricing system for teaching. Partial leveling down, such as significant rate capping, would also leave the private sector in a very difficult position. Severe damage to several of our greatest universities, caused by policies that prevent them from competing on the basis of quality in relation to cost, would be a national tragedy. The consequences would be felt for years to come.

What should be done? OMB ought to develop a comprehensive economic and policy model for research universities, and manage revisions in A-21 accordingly. The secretary of education and others concerned about private-sector tuition should start paying close attention to the debates within the government about A-21. Agency program officers, auditors, and negotiators should renew their commitment to investment in science, and stop viewing their activities as procurement. And school administrators should work with faculty to propagate an integrated and accurate view of the way economics and program objectives intersect in the modern research university.

The most helpful outcome, however, would be for the Congress and the administration to agree to fund scientific research adequately, and not try to squeeze university researchers with monopsonistic power. The federal government must take a long-term policy perspective on the maintenance of our research capacity and our graduate training programs. How well the United States competes in the next century will depend to a considerable degree on the policies we make today.

4

FUNDING
INSTRUCTION

FRANK B. CAMPANELLA

W HEN speaking of capital financing for colleges and universities, it is unlikely that a more comprehensive catalog of both new and tried techniques exists than Anderson and Meyerson's report.[1] Physical and financial capital needs are explored in depth, as are variations of post-tax reform means of debt, equity, and tuition financing. Given that full agenda, limited consideration is given to the financing of the human capital of faculty, staff, researchers, and the instruction of students, all so critical to the aspirations of our colleges and universities.

Moreover, current studies may have concentrated too much on research universities. While our national competitiveness is linked to research carried out in a select number of universities, it is also tied to the development of international sophistication in new generations of students. Instruction in language, area studies, and international business as well as in cross-cultural studies will critically affect our nation's standing in a global economy.

In developing the topic of funding for instruction, we must return to planning for the costs of operations and their financing.

1. Richard E. Anderson and Joel W. Meyerson, eds., *Financing Higher Education: Strategies After Tax Reform* (San Francisco: Jossey–Bass, 1987).

This chapter will draw heavily on the experiences of Boston College.

___ FACULTY SALARIES

Financing

Few would argue with the proposition that faculty are the essence of the academic enterprise. The ability to attract and retain top-quality faculty is in no small measure dependent on salary policy and working conditions. These factors in turn drive what is the largest single expenditure for most institutions— faculty salaries and benefits. In a typical academic department, faculty salaries might well account for 75 to 85 percent of the budget. Not surprisingly, considerable effort is expended to monitor, model, manage, and massage information about faculty and their salaries. We will return to this element of the equation.

The majority of private institutions look first to tuition revenues to fund faculty salaries. This is not likely to change significantly in the foreseeable future. It must be recognized as well that the financing of faculty salaries with restricted or unrestricted gift income, or from payout from the endowment, is highly institutional-specific.

Boston College suffered severe operating deficits in the late 1960s and early 1970s. Of necessity, operational control leading to surpluses was achieved rather quickly. The strategy for the last fifteen years has been to maintain tight cost control, establish faculty salary increases as a budget priority, and generate surpluses, in order to strengthen the balance sheet:

- To restore liquid and real assets that had been used up to finance prior deficits.
- To eliminate an excessive amount of unattractive short-term debt.
- To reverse a negative fund balance in the current fund.

The academic enterprise has been almost totally financed with tuition revenues during this time period. Unrestricted gift income has fallen to the bottom line, as a surplus of revenues over expenditures, and is an essential part of the strategy to accomplish longer-term financial objectives.

At this point in time, with a healthy balance sheet, and with growing internal and external pressures for restraining tuition growth rates, the proportion of the instructional budget funded with unrestricted gift income is likely to increase at Boston College. While it is difficult to generalize here, it does appear that pressures to limit tuition growth will place greater demands on the use of unrestricted gift income to fund current operations in those institutions not already employing all such funds for this purpose.

Similarly, the availability of income from endowment to support faculty salaries and other instructional costs varies widely among the institutions of higher education. Although much has been written about portfolio management and the payout problem, relatively few institutions possess endowment funds of sufficient magnitude to make a difference. The National Association of College and University Business Officers conducts an annual endowment survey. The 1988 survey included the endowment market value of 38 institutions of higher education in New England and New York. Approximately 71 percent of the total market value of these endowments was concentrated in five institutions; half of the institutions owned 90 percent of the total endowment funds.

Again using Boston College as an example, in 1973 the restricted endowment was $5 million. Because endowment income on an insignificant endowment is trivial, and *any* level of payout is negligible when compared with the size of the operating budget, the decision was made to invest the endowment funds for maximum capital gains. Today the endowment, including quasi endowment funds, is $200 million, and the institution is considering a limited payout from new capital fund raising for faculty salaries, scholarships, and new capital additions. Here again the degree to which endowments can support faculty salaries and other instructional costs is highly institution-specific.

59

Trends

Although new opportunities for financing faculty salaries are at best limited, the upward pressures on faculty salaries and benefits will continue to be significant. The harnessing of inflation has helped institutions of higher education make significant progress. Nevertheless, the salaries of those in the teaching professions are considerably below those in other professions. New national initiatives to attract top-quality students into the field of teaching will be felt both directly and indirectly in the budgets of academe, as will the rightful forces to end both sex and age discrimination in salary and benefit practices and policies.

Current experience with faculty shortages in selected areas (physical sciences, finance, computer science) prefigures the more general shortages expected in the next decade. Summer research stipends, reduced teaching loads, and budgets to reequip laboratories typically accompany high starting salaries for new faculty hired in these disciplines. There is little reason to expect moderation of these cost pressures when a more general shortage of faculty is anticipated. This is common knowledge to most campus leaders. Yet antithetically it is "business as usual" on most campuses.

Although it is tautological that financing faculty salaries is a function of the total dollar value of the salaries to be financed, it is important to understand the elements that determine that amount. In aggregate, faculty salaries are determined by salary levels and by the number of faculty on the payroll.

This chapter proposes two initiatives at the campus level to bring better understanding of the forces that drive aggregate faculty salaries—in terms of salary levels and numbers of faculty required to accomplish the teaching and scholarly objectives of the institution. For the former, better tools are required to measure salary levels compared with those of like institutions, and compared with inflation indices. For the latter, it is necessary to revisit the disciplines of cost and productivity analyses.

Competitive Levels

At Boston College there is a published goal of maintaining faculty salaries in the top quartile of the 168 Category I institutions listed in the annual report of the American Association of University Professors (AAUP). Between 1986 and 1987, at the associate professor level, Boston College's ranking dropped from the 80th to the 70th percentile. The proposed faculty solution to the problem was straightforward: Add an amount to next year's budget that is determined by multiplying the number of associates by the dollar differential between the 70th and 80th percentiles. Although this solution is straightforward, it is also costly and perhaps erroneous.

In this instance we do not know that the decile ranking is correct. Determining the actual percentile ranking of an institution, using the quintile summary statistics published by AAUP, is hazardous, given the relative flatness of the "Salary v. Institutional Ranking curve. Although it is a simple matter to request *decile* data (by category of institution, by faculty rank), it is also easy using a personal computer to enter the salary data by faculty rank for all institutions in a given category and then sort by salary. Not only does this provide the correct ranking, it identifies one's neighbors in the ranking and their comparative salaries in a much more useful format than the alpha listing by state provided in the AAUP report.[2]

It should be noted too, that these AAUP rankings depend not only on the university's salary policy, but also on its promotion policy. When a senior associate professor is promoted to full professor, the average for the associate professor rank loses a high salary while the average for the full professor rank gains a junior salary. In isolation, this action lowers the average salaries of both ranks. At Boston College there has been significant movement up through the ranks in the past decade. There are 25 percent more full professors, 64 percent more associates, and 30 percent fewer

2. "The Annual Report on the Economic Status of the Profession 1986–87," *ACADEME*, Bulletin of the American Association of University Professors, (March–April, 1987).

assistant professors. This compares with an increase in total faculty of just 10 percent.

Finally, the competitive standing of average salaries in the rank of assistant professor in particular depends not only on salary policy, but also on market factors. Many new assistant professors, for example, were hired in the fall of 1988. Their distribution over various disciplines and the related market-driven variations in starting salaries, by discipline, will have an impact on the average salary reported for assistant professors.

At the institutional level, at least, it would appear desirable to understand the impact of promotion and hiring policies on competitive salary rankings, if these are to influence salary policy decisions. This is easily accomplished. By developing a faculty flow model over time, we can examine average salaries by rank, and the relative impact of forces that drive them (number of faculty, total salaries of new hires, promotions-in, promotions-out, and departures). When making comparisons across institutions, the isolation of salary decisions appears to be adequately accomplished through the comparison of percent changes in salaries by rank for continuing faculty. These comparative data are available in the AAUP report.

Inflation

A favorite pastime of faculty salary committees, academic managers, and professional organizations is to fret about levels of faculty salaries relative to inflation indices such as the consumer price index (CPI) or GNP deflator. Although average salary data in this instance may be useful to professional organizations, it is inadequate for making informed management decisions at the institutional level. Not only are the averages influenced by the hiring market and promotion decisions noted above, but when used over time, they include an unknown number of faculty who are no longer at the institution.

To overcome some of these difficulties, Boston College uses an annual faculty cohort study for measuring changes in salaries in relation to changes in the CPI. A faculty cohort is defined by date-of-hire. Today's cohorts include only the persisters, those faculty hired over the last four decades who are still aboard.

A typical cohort is made up of the faculty hired in 1978–79. As of 1988, there were seventeen faculty remaining in that cohort. When hired in September of 1978, their total salaries were $256,600. In 1988 their salaries were $679,800. This represents an average annual compound growth of 10.1 percent per year, or a percent change of 161 percent. During that time period, 1978 to 1988, the CPI increased from 202.1 to 360.9 for an average annual compound growth of 6.0 percent per year or a percent change of 78.6 percent. So it is readily seen that the salary increases provided to this cohort did handily outpace the rate of inflation. Similar calculations are carried out for each cohort hired over the past thirty years and the study is updated annually.

In the 1988–89 study, there is not a single case where salaries have not outperformed the CPI. And so the perennial concern about keeping pace with inflation is put to rest at the outset. The study is, however, what it purports to be and nothing more. It concerns itself solely with the cost-of-living component of salary changes for the faculty at the institution today. The study does not address salary increases for either merit or promotion, although the fact that salary increases exceeded increases in the inflation index suggests that funds were distributed to the persisters for these purposes.

Cost and Productivity Analyses

In the naïve and ready acceptance of a myriad of management techniques in the late 1960s and early 1970s, managers in the academy were frequently disappointed. It was eventually recognized that purveyors of materials, conferences, and consulting services for PPBS, MBO, long-range planning, ZBB, cost analyses, and "totally integrated" MIS were accomplishing little more than lining their own coffers at the expense of the colleges. The failure of these programs to address the managerial problems and concerns of our institutions led eventually to a whole-sale rejection of the management "alphabet." A residual skepticism remains, and for the most part is no doubt a healthy one.

Perhaps in the area of cost analysis we threw the "baby out with the bath water." In the late 1960s and early 1970s there were many attitudinal, political, logistical, managerial, and institutional reasons for not embracing studies of costs and productivity. It does, however, seem time to return to these efforts. Certainly, if faculty salaries and benefits continue under great pressure and if these comprise the largest single component of our budgets, there is a rationale for understanding them, and a companion obligation to manage them. But even these arguments pale in the light of the *Second Law of Costing:* Rising costs in the context of stable and possibly declining revenues and their joint consequences make the need for cost analysis self-evident, even to the skeptics.

In 1982 Boston College began "Cost and Productivity" studies of every department on campus, both academic and administrative. The proximate cause was trustee concern for productivity. Although the student enrollment peaked at 14,000 in 1976, annual budgets, without exception, called for extraordinary cost increases, most related to increased staffing levels for both faculty and for all other employee categories.

It was understood that to be successful this work must be done sensitively, with an understanding of the academic environment and with the cooperation of the responsible manager or department chair in each instance. It was important to communicate at the outset just how these cost studies would be used. Most important, we attempted to communicate trustee and management understanding of some of the limitations of such studies.

"Guidelines for Interpreting the Cost and Productivity Studies" were sent to the department chairs well in advance of the study itself. The guidelines described the purposes of the studies, the methodology, and how the results would be used. The costing methodologies used in the guidelines were developed with accounting and finance faculty in the School of Management and revised after applying the procedures to the School of Management itself. This document became the basis for initial discussions between the financial analyst and the department chair. The interested reader is referred to an article published by the Society for College and University Planning for a detailed description of costing methodologies employed by Boston College for both Academic and Administrative Departments.[3]

After the program had been in place for six months, five departments, on their own initiative, had requested productivity studies. The most notable success, though, came in the form of a letter received from the warrior chieftain of the Chemistry Department soon after the completion of a cost and productivity study of his area.

This chairman had begun the process by stating that no one conducting a cost analysis could possibly account for the complexities of a department involved in graduate and undergraduate teaching, laboratory and classroom instruction, and commitments to research, sponsored and unsponsored.

> Now that the productivity study on the Chemistry Department is complete and my motives for writing are thus no longer attributable to self-interest, I just wanted you to know that I think [the staff member who performed the study] is really first-rate. I found her to be smart, thorough, and perceptive. She also listens well, appreciates subtleties, and does her homework. In short, she left me with the strong impression that, although she is hardly a pushover, we had been treated fairly. I don't envy her assignment in the least, but I'm hard pressed to imagine that you could find anyone to handle it better.

Clearly it makes managerial sense to carry out such studies. This paper argues that the time has come to revisit the discipline of costing in our institutions. With proper preparation, the involvement of the right people in the conduct of the studies,

3. Eileen M. Gaffney, "Cost and Productivity Analysis for Higher Education," *Planning for Higher Education,* Society for College and University Planning, 16:1, (1987–1988).

and attention to the concerns of department chairs, it can be done.

___ FINANCING EQUIPMENT

The financing of equipment in an era of rapid technological change presents a whole set of financial challenges. Historically, the equipment-intensive departments in institutions of higher education have been the physical sciences, audio-visual services, the computing center, and, sometimes, the psychology department. Changes in technology have had a dual impact on these departments. New technologies, such as Nuclear Magnetic Resonance (NMR), require the purchase of new advanced scientific instrumentation, whereas changes in technology (for example, diffractometers) render existing equipment obsolete.

Simultaneously, developments in communications and computing technologies, which have created the information age, are critical to colleges and universities. Our strategic business is information. We create it, store it, retrieve it, and share it in all its many forms, from knowledge on the high end, to information at a midpoint, to raw unprocessed data ready for study and research at a lower level. Information is our only business, more so than it is that of an IBM or DEC or Apple, as hardware manufacturers, or Lotus and Execucom as software developers.

The implications of rapid technological change for equipment budgets are dramatic. Not only have the science departments become even more intensive users, as has audio-visual services, but brand new intensive-use departments have been created. The library is a prime example, but there is also the computer science department, the accounting and math departments, the economics department, and, to a lesser but not insignificant extent, the academic departments of the social sciences and humanities.

At Boston College, the annual capital budget (not including new construction) has grown by 135 percent since 1982. Three-fourths of this growth has funded computing and communica-

66

tions equipment and projects. Those elements in the same time period have grown from 15 to 40 percent of the annual capital budget.

The Director of Information Technology Services at B.C. offers the following reasons why costs in the information age will continue to climb:

> Overall spending will continue to escalate. With the levels of permeation that exist right now, there are a lot of financial people out there saying that although we spent a lot of money, it was short-term, and now it's going to flatten out. On the contrary, spending will continue to escalate.
>
> New products offer dramatic increases in speed, capacity, and capability, but at a slightly higher price. Vendors will try to increase sales by giving the buyer more for his money, but what they will not do is offer the older machines for less money. There will be more for the money, but there will be increased spending on a single unit.
>
> Faculty and staff expect a microcomputer as a normal tool in the performance of their jobs, and institutions are expected to shoulder most of the cost. As technologies merge, the product that somebody is using becomes part of a network: it's in the office, it's used for work, people send messages on it, it accesses host data bases, and it performs transaction processing. The user is going to believe that the product is every bit as much a part of the job as the telephone.
>
> More of the dollars spent on micros are allocated to upgrades and add-ons than to new stations. At first, during the big flurry of microcomputer activity, a high percentage of spending was on new units, but that proportion has been reversed.[4]
>
> Technological life-cycles are growing shorter, resulting in more frequent shifts in equipment or upgrades. For example, the 3270 terminals installed over ten years ago are still churning away. But for micros, it is not unusual to go through a total replacement with upgrades for something that is not more than two years old.
>
> Early users of technology are likely to be the most knowledgeable and will want to move to the next generation. The migration is

4. At Boston College today, permeation of micros within the faculty is 75 percent. Approximately 50 percent of the budget is spent for replacement and upgrades with the balance spent on new systems.

already under way. There are a lot of people on our campuses now who were the early adopters of technology—they were the most innovative, and they were the most comfortable with it. People might think that since Professor A was given a micro two years ago, that should take care of him for a long time. Actually, that person is likely to be the most aggressive in acquiring new and better equipment.[5]

Not to be overlooked in the consideration of factors that drive equipment costs are the significant new costs for maintenance and user support. Maintenance is now growing in proportion to expenditures for equipment. It is hoped that with more reliable equipment and more experienced users, maintenance will level off and perhaps decline slightly as a proportion of the hardware-software-user support cost mix. User support is now increasing exponentially relative to expenditures for equipment. With the advent of readily accessible network computing services and the increase of experienced (if not sophisticated) users, it may be reasonable to hypothesize a decline in user support services as a proportion of this mix. But do not look for this tomorrow— perhaps in the early to mid-1990s.

So, as in the case of financing faculty salaries, it is easier to identify pressures on the cost side of the equation than to imagine creative responses that will finance the resultant cost increases. There are, however, some new opportunities.

Many new and profitable companies provide hardware and software to colleges and universities. At the same time, higher education is considered a large and attractive market segment to many of these companies. The confluence of these factors can provide unique opportunities for corporate support for on-campus initiatives in computing and communications.

Corporations surely recognize that student turnover makes colleges and universities a continuously refreshed market. Nor are they unaware of the advantage of developing product loyalty among students who are initiated in the use of a particular piece of hardware or software. Although somewhat lagging, corpora-

5. Bernard M. Gleason, in *The EDUTECH Report* (Bloomfield, CT: Edutech International, 1986).

tions appear to be learning that the diversity of our institutions translates to some very strong market subsegments, each with its own traits, problems, and opportunities. Should corporate appreciation for such relatively independent subsegments continue to develop, we might well experience a more level playing field for financing opportunities, represented by gifts and gifts-in-kind than has been traditional in general corporate giving and in the allocation of research funds.

There is a variety of methods to develop cooperative relationships with these corporations. Most colleges and universities, through alumni, development offices, trustees, chambers of commerce, and other means, have been doing it for years. There are now new opportunities to develop proposals that will generate gifts or gifts-in-kind to support the financing of computing and communications equipment.

EQUIPMENT DEPRECIATION

For the past twelve years Boston College has followed the practice of depreciating all its equipment, library holdings, and real assets. Depreciation is calculated straight-line, on the basis of cost, for the estimated life of the asset. An amount equal to the total depreciation is budgeted each year in the Current Fund and a cash transfer in this amount is made to the Plant Fund. There the cash is used to pay principal on long-term debt and to fund renewals and replacements (including equipment replacement) in the capital budget. Amounts of depreciation in excess of that used for principal payment and replacements are invested in the plant fund.

With this scheme in place there is no discomfort in financing the purchase of 200 Macintosh systems with 30-year tax-exempt debt. After three years (the estimated useful life of the Mac) the initial investment is recovered and the funds are in place to finance the purchase of the next generation of equipment. Although the resulting funds are net of principal repayment, the excess of depreciation over principal each year presumably has

69

been invested at market rates. Of course, in a closed, no-growth system, this will work only until the crossover where accelerating annual principal payments overtake the flat annual charge for depreciation. It is simple enough to model such a system relaxing the no-growth assumptions for both real and price growth, and using varying rates of return for invested funds.

The experience at Boston College is interesting. The first round of 128K Mac systems was purchased in 1984 for $1,372 for the Mac and an external disk drive. Two academic years later, these were replaced and resold to students and other members of the community for their personal use. Book value after two years was about $460. The systems on average required $40 of servicing (mouse replacements, etc.) and were sold for $570. In truth it was nothing more than serendipity that caused an overestimated useful life to be offset by an underestimated residual value. The bottom line was a net profit of $70 per system, and every system was sold.

One way to shift some of the burden for financing this equipment is to require students to purchase personal computers. That strategy, however, is not without problems. Had we done that at Boston College, as the Mac computer evolved, the senior class would be using 128K Macs, the juniors 512K Macs, the sophomores the MacPlus, and some freshmen would be purchasing SEs and IIs. It would be hard to know just what faculty and department secretaries would be using. But even with a requirement to purchase, institutions must maintain significant public facilities for students to run common software, which their personal computers might not handle. Presumably the machines and software in public facilities and in the hands of faculty and departments would be replaced or upgraded in lockstep.

Another strategy, somewhat less restrictive and perhaps more expensive, is to encourage the voluntary purchase of personal computers. The Boston College Computer Store sells Macs, other equipment, and software at cost to faculty and with minimal markup (less than 10 percent) to students. There are extensive public facilities as well. The long-term strategy is to offload selected heavy student users when those public facilities reach capacity. At that time, MBAs, computer science, and math majors may be required to purchase computers.

⎯ CONCLUSION

It is startling to realize just how much easier it is to recognize the serious pressures that will continue to drive instructional costs upward than it is to identify creative or new means to generate the required financing.

The response then is a predictable one. It involves providing financing by pushing traditional funding sources as hard as possible. And it calls for control and discipline on the cost side, in order to insure that all of these funds are spent as effectively as possible.

5

USING DEBT
EFFECTIVELY

ROBERT T. FORRESTER

FROM 1981 to 1986, colleges and universities floated an estimated $20 billion of tax-exempt debt. Effective use of debt has become one of the most significant tasks of college and university financial executives. It involves:

- Obtaining and maintaining financing at the lowest cost.
- Preserving institutional debt capacity for periods of special need.
- Balancing maturity risks between short- and long-term debt.
- Matching sources of funding with particular projects.
- Assuring that departments and schools that incur debt make appropriate budgetary plans.
- Scanning world economic trends to minimize risks and costs.

These issues are the focus of this chapter, which examines debt and other funding issues at three universities—Brown, Harvard, and Kentucky.*

* This chapter draws heavily from the panelists at the Annapolis symposium: Jack C. Blanton of the University of Kentucky, Frederick Bohen of Brown

Some higher education officials believe that colleges and universities should have as little debt as possible. Debt avoidance may be desirable if institutions have unlimited access to nondebt capital. In the real world, however, this view is unnecessarily restrictive and may be counterproductive. Commercial institutions that rigidly avoid debt can miss opportunities for leverage and innovation. Similarly, colleges with a conservative position on debt may not have the resources to breathe new life into existing or newly created programs. For those institutions that are debt-averse but have an obvious need for borrowing, a simple rule may be to cut back on weak programs and redirect the newly freed institutional resources to fund the debt service. For other institutions—those with a mixture of debt and equity and those that must rely on borrowing—the key is to force debt service into the budget so that it must compete with other expenditures.

"Using debt effectively" means different things to these three universities. Although all institutions have significant levels of debt, their approaches to debt financing are quite different. These philosophies are shaped by past experience and different financial contexts. Brown draws down debt with trepidation; Harvard finances capital renovation with a mix of debt and its substantial equity; and Kentucky traditionally borrows for most of its campus improvements.

Students in a college finance course may imagine that debt management is a process of determining an ideal capital structure and planning and directing the various flows of financial resources to achieve that structure. In reality, as these three institutions how, planning occurs on a department-by-department or project-by-project basis. The resulting financial structure is measured from time to time against some guidelines, which may not always be clearly defined. Perhaps this is because, in the past, many colleges and certainly the state universities have had adequate debt capacity to finance their projects. Another reason may be the decentralized nature of operations in a

University, Robert Cenci of Goldman Sachs, and Robert Scott of Harvard University

74

large university. In such a structure, it may take a crisis, rather than formal advance planning, to produce the best solutions.

═ BROWN UNIVERSITY

Brief financial overview.   Brown University is the smallest of the three schools studied here. It has an annual operating budget of approximately $143 million, more than half of which is funded by tuition revenue. Of the balance, government grants provide 20 percent, gifts 12 to 13 percent, and investment income approximately 10 percent. Debt service is about 2.5 percent of educational and general expenses and about 6 percent of auxiliary expenses. Indebtedness for plant is about $78 million or one-third of capitalization.

Use of debt and other forms of funding.   For the larger problems of universities, crises produce solutions. Crisis is often more important than the best techniques and planning because, in the absence of crisis, planning is not pursued energetically. Brown's crisis came in the 1970s. Like many institutions, Brown was caught by the rapid escalation of prices, a weak stock market, and its own reluctance to raise tuition. Like many other colleges and universities, Brown experienced deficits and drew down on reserves.

The trauma of the 1970s is reflected in Brown's attitude today toward debt. For a time in the late 1970s, the university was shut out of the debt market. Later, when finances stabilized, the board strongly resisted assuming additional debt. This antipathy toward borrowing continues to the present and has both negative and positive implications for Brown's future.

On the downside, a reluctance to borrow has limited the resources available to the university. Valuable projects have sat "on the shelf" when they could have contributed to the quality and effectiveness of programs. Deferred maintenance costs exceed $60 million for 137 campus buildings. Urgent, in some cases program-threatening, needs of $25 to 28 million were identified for the board. The board chose to use almost the entire endowment income of $12 million to address the highest priority needs systematically. Soft money was another source of funds for expansion. New debt was avoided at all costs.

On the positive side, the university is now reasonably financially sound. For the past five years, the university has had budget surpluses between 2 and 3 percent. Each of these unanticipated surpluses has been dedicated to small capital improvement projects. The austere budgets forced administrators to seek creative and inexpensive solutions to problems: Brown greatly expanded its information technology programs and facilities through donated equipment.

Comment. Perhaps the most valuable result of Brown's policy is ironic. Even though Brown had to avoid new borrowing, the university now has some debt capacity. The more moderate current debt level gives university administrators some cushion when facing the economic uncertainties of the 1990s.

Brown, however, has not fully escaped from its financial overcommitment of the 1970s. It faces major capital needs that are exacerbated by the institution's inability to borrow in the last decade. Brown must modernize or replace large medical, engineering, and information technology facilities. With the second highest student charges in the Ivy League, tuition cannot be considered an expandable revenue source. External fund raising rose from $7 million in 1977 to $51 million in 1987, but the university administration does not think it can sustain that rate of growth over the next ten years.

Thus, Brown faces some difficult choices in the next few years. The university is committed to quality with fiscal conservatism. This may require pruning out of the rich field of activities those older programs that have outlived their usefulness or newer programs that have not lived up to a once-bright promise. Any expansion or even maintenance of the status quo would require a substantial tuition hike, a dramatic increase in fund-raising performance, or increased debt. Impractical or distasteful as these alternatives may be, they could be the only alternatives to program contraction as Brown enters the 1990s.

___ HARVARD UNIVERSITY

Brief financial overview. Harvard is probably the most thoroughly analyzed institution of higher education in America. This statistical summary, therefore, will restrict itself to general budget data and the budget process.

Harvard's annual budget exceeds $800 million. The budget of one of its schools, the Harvard Business School's $100 million plus, is larger than the total budgets of many universities. And its debt burden is similarly immense: at the end of 1987, it carried $782 million of unrefunded debt on its books. Of the total indebtedness, $400 million is academic debt, and the debt service on the academic debt alone is 4 to 5 percent of the university's operating budget.

Harvard has both short-term (one year) and long-term (five to ten years) budgeting processes. Budgets are prepared on a department-by-department basis, and the university budget is the sum of its departments' budgets. Occasionally, the board makes major decisions on the scale and scope of programs, but in general it defers to the departments for budgets and planning. The dean and his or her staff in each school are responsible for planning how they are going to achieve the academic objectives that the dean and board have agreed upon. The resulting budget includes all the formal operating expenses, and all supporting expenses that are allocated to the school.

Major differences exist among the schools, and, consequently, major differences exist among the schools' budgets and plans. For example, the business and law schools, which are supported primarily by current fees and contributions, draw relatively few funds from endowment. The Faculty of Arts and Sciences, on the other hand, relies heavily on endowment support.

Use of debt and other forms of funding. Harvard steers a middle path between the debt-aversion of Brown and the debt-orientation of Kentucky.

As noted above, budget and planning are decentralized at Harvard. After the deans prepare their individual school's bud-

77

gets, the central administration and board must make some decisions. Based on each individual school's budget and plan, the central administration projects future capital requirements for each unit and in the aggregate. If the school does not have adequate funds from current fees and gifts to finance a particular requirement, the administration then faces the basic question, "What is the cheapest way to finance the requirement?"

Often, fund raising is the preferred means. Recently, Harvard had a problem of deteriorating facilities in the medical school. The facility question was closely related to curricular issues on better ways of teaching medicine. The medical school determined that it needed to raise $200 million to ease the problems. The Kennedy School of Government provides another example of preference for fund raising. This school has grown tremendously since the 1970s, in part as the result of substantial investment of the president's time in fund raising. What was once a small department now has a $30 million annual budget. These two examples suggest that fund raising may be a preferred funding mechanism for a major capital development or start-up funding of a new program.

Harvard uses debt where there is a relatively flexible fee structure to help repay it, or for those activities, such as facilities renovation and building, where there are financial or tax advantages. Harvard used tax-exempt debt heavily in the 1980s for facilities renovation. Very few buildings were constructed and the university has almost no building plans for the foreseeable future. But facilities renovation has a high priority at Harvard, with school budgets that are expected to carry full costs of depreciation.

Comment. Harvard was very fortunate to borrow heavily during the recent period of relatively cheap debt, prior to the tax reform volume caps. The University was able to renovate many facilities at much lower cost than would be possible today. But Harvard, like most institutions, still faces a severe problem of plant deterioration. Its 70 million square feet has a replacement value of over $3 billion. Assuming that the average campus building has a useful life of 40 years, replacement-cost-based depreciation should be $80 million. This sum, equal to 10 percent of the current operating budget, is more than twice as much as the university actually allocates. There is no clear solution to this problem, but Harvard's practice of mandatory depreciation of facilities in each school budget is a useful step in clarifying the problem and should be carefully considered by other universities.

UNIVERSITY OF KENTUCKY

Brief financial overview. Kentucky is a comprehensive public research university with a medical center, a hospital, graduate and undergraduate colleges, and a number of professional schools including medicine, dentistry, allied health, engineering, education, agriculture, and law. Its education and general (E&G) budget is approximately $400 million a year. About 60 percent of the E&G budget comes from state appropriations. Total indebtedness at the end of fiscal year 1986 was $145 million, plus $21 million in hospital bonds. The reasons for incurring the debt include: $82 million for the construction and renovation of academic buildings of the main university; $33 million for dining facilities and dormitories; $28 million for the community college facilities (these are considered part of the university); and $2 million for other purposes. The debt structure is approximately 25 percent debt and 75 percent equity. Available funds from unrestricted plant, quasi endowment, and current funds are approximately equal to the debt.

Use of debt and other forms of financing. At Kentucky, revenue debt is the *only* effective form of debt financing. For many years Kentucky had limited resources and considered itself a poor state. This self-image affected all branches of state government, including the state university. One consequence of this image is that *institutionally incurred* debt (although still under the umbrella of the state) is the primary source of capital financing.

Historically, the Commonwealth of Kentucky has favored

revenue debt financing. This is rooted in the state constitution. Kentucky's constitution requires the commonwealth to seek voter approval for all general obligation (GO) debt over $500,000. Obviously, this tends to inhibit GO debt. So, virtually all state capital projects are funded with revenue debt financing. While the University's debt level is comparable to Brown's and Harvard's, it is high for a public institution. It is more common for states to use GO debt (which will appear on the state's, not the university's balance sheet) to finance general academic buildings. Today the Commonwealth of Kentucky has the highest per capita revenue debt in the nation.

The university administration submits capital project requests to the legislative state council on higher education and the the governor's office. The governor then formulates a budget plan that is sent to the legislature. The general assembly calculates how much debt service is required to fund the projects. If the legislature feels that it can appropriate sufficient money from the general fund on a recurring basis, then the projects are approved. University revenue bonds for academic purposes are secured by pledges of the tuition for those programs. Bonds for auxiliary purposes are secured as they are in other states.

Comment. Just as Brown faces some difficulties by its avoidance of debt, Kentucky's more open embrace of debt leads to complications—especially for a public institution. The most immediate effect is felt in the annual appropriation process. Debt service is one more line item in the university's budget proposal to the legislature. But, in effect, this line subordinates all other line item requests as it represents an unavoidable commitment. In years of plenty, the other lines (such as salaries) will receive adequate funding. But when state revenues are in tight supply and the budget is squeezed, the debt service may consume a disproportionate share of the pie.

This situation also highlights a common problem in all debt financing: There is no foolproof formula for calculating maximum debt capacity. Kentucky is able to handle its current debt load, but there appears to be no restraint on the growth of debt. Debt service could continue to rise both in volume and as a

percentage of total expenditures. At some point, possibly has-
tened by a sudden shift in the economy, debt service may over-
whelm the other budget items with devastating consequences for
the academic programs of the university. University officials,
when they are considering the issuance of revenue debt, must
keep a watchful eye on the Kentucky economy, which is, of course,
linked to the national economy. And our national economy is
increasingly dependent on decisions made in Bonn and Tokyo.

― SOME CONCLUDING OBSERVATIONS

Traditionally, colleges have had three choices when considering capital plans: (1) don't build, (2) build with debt, or (3) build
with cash. For some colleges only the first two alternatives are
real. The University of Kentucky is in this situation because it
does not have access to the public treasury for capital projects.
For other universities, like Brown or Harvard, with a large pool
of equity in the form of endowment or a coalition of donors, the
third choice is equally real.

On a project-by-project basis the important choice is between building and not building, and that decision comes from a
sound capital budgeting process. The choice between debt and
cash depends on the expected return on cash, the interest rate on
debt, and the proportion of interest that can be recovered from
the college's revenue sources.

Some institutions that have debt (or are about to acquire
debt) are establishing guidelines that clearly define debt policies
and procedures, though most, like the three cases described
above, have no formal rules. The first guideline an institution
should follow is that it seek the lowest *overall* cost of capital. If
tax-exempt debt costs 8 percent and endowment funds earn 5
percent, debt may appear too expensive. But for an institution
receiving 12 to 15 percent total return on endowment, debt may
be very attractive. A better decision criterion might be the return
on fixed income securities in the endowment portfolio. Now that
several large private universities are precluded from entering the

tax-exempt market, their investment managers might actively consider internal capital needs as an alternative fixed-income investment, with the operating budget providing a return to the endowment. Regardless of the institution's credit rating, there is no default risk to the endowment for this type of internally directed "investment."

Second, management should balance the need for an affordable cost of capital with the desire to have each project stand on its own. In some cases, colleges have decided to incur debt only for those projects that generate incremental revenue. This will raise questions, for example, about how to build classroom debt service into the operating budget.

Third, management and the board of trustees have to weigh their position on interest rate risk. One college could decide that long assets, such as plant, should be balanced only with long-term debt. Under this policy, program notes might be appropriate. But management would not want to roll them over forever. The decision to take advantage of attractive short-term rates should be based on liquidity and the availability of credit support. A more important consideration may be the current interest-rate environment. The 1990s, as the first chapter observes, could bring double-digit inflation (which would effectively relieve the burden of debt from everyone with fixed-interest debt) or the decade could bring a recession perhaps caused by a trade war, which typically brings lower interest rates. In any event, the prospects for interest-rate instability are high. Consequently, the costs of interest-rate caps and swaps may be low in comparison to the protection they can provide in this type of economy.

Fourth, the continuing regulatory threats to tax-exempt financing should be carefully weighed.

Fifth, the appropriation and financing decisions—and approvals—should be separate. Debt, like contributed or earned equity, should be used only to finance projects that could otherwise stand on their own.

And sixth, an institution should consider limits on its absolute debt exposure. Regardless of how desirable particular projects may be, a university may not wish to take them on if additional debt threatens its viability.

Some observers believe that, despite borrowing billions in the 1981–86 period, universities are substantially "underborrowed." It is very difficult to determine the debt capacity of a particular institution. Chapter 7 reviews many of the important elements to be considered. Yet even the universities that are most heavily indebted, like Harvard and Stanford, are considered highly credit-worthy for additional debt issues. Clearly each educational institution, like each corporation, must become comfortable that its debt load is consistent with its financial and operating strategy.

6

TAXABLE

FINANCING

ARTHUR J. KALITA

T HE Tax Reform Act of 1986 had a massive effect on tax-exempt financing by colleges and universities. After tax reform, higher education administrators and their bankers have had to redesign strategies for raising capital. Of the financing alternatives available, taxable debt may assume new importance to issuers seeking ways to meet their capital needs.

However, it will take time for the taxable markets to understand and accept issuers who traditionally have borrowed in the tax-exempt markets. All parties to these new transactions must be educated: Higher education administrators must learn the basics of the taxable markets, while underwriters and investors must grow accustomed to analyzing financial statements based on fund accounting rather than traditional corporate accounting.

For higher education issuers, the taxable market not only differs in costs from the tax-exempt market, but is fundamentally different in kind and scope. The taxable market is vastly greater in size, and the available products are both more numerous and more flexible than the tax-exempt products. The tax-exempt market functions almost exclusively within the context of the American national economy, and tax-exempt securities offer few advantages to nondomestic individuals or corporations. But in today's global economy, one cannot speak of taxable domestic markets without referring to the worldwide taxable markets. Later, we will examine both the domestic and the global taxable markets.

The market for higher education taxable issues is still very small. Only $139.4 million of taxable bonds were issued for educational purposes between fall of 1985 and fall of 1987 (excluding student loan agencies). Nevertheless, as this volume increases, issuers can expect an increase in numbers and greater standardization of taxable vehicles, enabling both increased liquidity and more efficient pricing.

Understanding and exploiting taxable markets should be understood by higher education administrators to involve more than interim solutions to current capital requirements. Both the U.S. Treasury and Congress are attempting to control the volume of tax-exempt debt. The 1988 decision of the U.S. Supreme Court in the State of South Carolina *v*. James A. Baker, III, casts doubt in the constitutional protection of the states to determine the uses of tax-exempt debt, leaving that prerogative to the Congress. Regardless of future amendments to the Internal Revenue Code, though, the need to issue taxable securities will grow. As long as tax-exempt debt continues to trade at a lower yield than Treasuries, tax-exempt obligations will be the cheapest source of funds to issuers. However, the future yields in tax-exempt markets are difficult to predict because tax reform also made tax-exempts less desirable to several classes of investors.

As spreads between the two markets continue to narrow, the advantages of taxable financing may begin to outweigh the higher interest costs. In some circumstances, taxable financing, even though at a higher cost of capital, may be less expensive than drawing on internal funds. The cost of external taxable debt may be less than the rate of return on endowment income. And for liquidity purposes, an institution may decide to borrow rather than use endowment for capital improvements.

THE NEED FOR ISSUING
TAXABLE DEBT

Four factors should be considered by higher educations issuers in issuing taxable debt:

- Increasing funding needs.
- Changes in the tax-exempt market.
- Legal constraints on tax-exempt debt
- Tactical and product advantages of taxable debt.

Increasing Funding Needs

Tax reform affected many traditional sources of higher education funding: access to tax-exempt markets was restricted, the after-tax cost of charitable giving increased, and limitations on credits for basic research activities were imposed. Tax reform did not alter the demand for funds. On the contrary, changes affecting individual savings and the taxation of scholarships and fellowships will in many cases increase demand for financial aid. As competition for students increases, colleges and universities will have to increase their spending per student, on everything from teachers' salaries to new construction, just to maintain their current positions academically. Overall, current higher educational aggregate capital needs are estimated at $45 to $50 billion, and some analysts have suggested that this figure covers only deferred maintenance.

David Halpern's 1987 study of college and university physical plants highlighted the demand for construction funds. Based on a representative sample of colleges and universities, the study showed that 60 percent of the institutions surveyed viewed rehabilitation/alteration of campus facilities as at least "extremely" or "very" urgent, and 26 percent more considered it "somewhat" urgent. In addition, 62 percent believed that new construction/additions were of similar urgency. "Obtaining

87

funds for upgrading and maintenance" was rated by respondents as the biggest challenge ahead. Although real expected costs are elusive, some analysts predict an annual need of $4 to $5 billion for physical plant maintenance and development. In a period of rising construction costs, these expenses will strain university resources.

Because rating agencies and investors examine student demand statistics and the conditions of physical plants, resources must be deployed to attract students and maintain the campus. An emerging paradox of funding facing higher education is the simultaneous need to raise capital to maintain an attractive campus knowing that the rating agencies may frown upon institutions with a relatively high debt load.

Changes in the Tax-Exempt Market

Neither investors nor issuers have been insulated from the impact of tax reform. As a result, the tax-exempt market has become more volatile and unpredictable. On the supply side, total volume has fallen because of market access limits or higher interest rates.

Reductions in supply should lead to better and more competitive pricing for the remaining issuers. However, the demand side of the market has also been radically altered. Elimination of the ability of commercial banks to deduct from taxable income the interest paid on borrowings for the purchase of tax-exempt bonds virtually eliminated banks as investors in the tax-exempt market. In addition, a significant reduction in demand was spurred by changes in personal income tax provisions that reduced the value of tax-exempt interest income to individuals and insurance companies. The net result of these changes has been increased volatility of the tax-exempt market. During 1987, it became painfully clear that the tax-exempt bond market was more volatile than the taxable market because of the narrowed investor base caused by tax reform.

Legal Constraints on Tax-Exempt Debt

The Tax Reform Act defined "private activity" by its use of proceeds, and developed two tests to determine private activity: a business use/security interest test and a private loan financing test. Because these tests pivot on "nongovernmental" usage definitions, the law is sweeping. Higher education institutions, as well as other 501 (c) 3 organizations, receive preferred status as "qualified 501 (c) 3 bonds, " although special rules governing tax-exempt offerings still preclude many colleges and universities from raising capital through tax-exempt debt.

Many regulations imposed by tax reform apply equally to public and private schools and agencies. However, private universities are subject to limits not applicable to state-supported schools. Universities that actively engage in cooperative efforts with private enterprise also face more difficulties in raising tax-exempt capital. Some of the more pronounced legal reasons for issuing taxable debt follow.

Volume caps. Both public and private colleges were omitted from the annual statewide unified volume ceiling limiting all tax-exempt private activity bonds to the greater of $75 per capita or $250 million of tax-exempt debt in 1987, and $50 per capita or $150 million after 1987. Private universities and colleges are subject to a separate volume cap of $150 million of qualified 501-(c)3 bonds outstanding per organization (including related organizations). This separate volume cap is important because it will increase costs for approximately 16 private universities which in 1987 had already passed the $150 million ceiling and must therefore rely on taxable borrowing. Institutions hovering in the $100 to $150 million range may soon face similar constraints. Student loan bonds are not charged against the institutions' $150 million cap.

Student loan bonds. The Tax Reform Act included student loan bonds within the annual statewide unified volume caps. These limits make future funding dependent on overall capital demands in the state. Thus there may be differences between states in allocating tax-exempt borrowing capacity to universities and agencies. Student loan tax-exempt bonds may be reduced as much as 50 percent, requiring many institutions to enter the taxable markets.

Qualified 501(c)3 bonds. To be a qualified 501(c)3 bond, two use-of-proceeds tests must be met. First, no more than 5 percent of the net bond proceeds may be applied toward "private activities" such as cafeterias, bookstores, laundries, parking facilities covered under leases, and long-term management or incentive pay contracts. Second, no more than 5 percent of debt service may be secured by or derived from an unrelated trade or business. Under a special separate ruling, in order for student loan bonds to be tax-exempt, no more than 10 percent of net proceeds can be used for nonstudent loan purposes. (The 10 percent limit applies only to bonds issued in conjunction with federal programs; bonds connected to state programs are limited to 5 percent.) Use of proceeds beyond the 5 or 10 percent limits will result in retroactive taxation of the issues.

Among the most affected institutions will be the research arms of public or private universities engaging in product research with private enterprise. Universities or colleges wishing to maintain these relationships will be forced to issue taxable debt for a project having a private activity purpose. Thus, the safer and more flexible course is the issuance of taxable bonds.

Financing bond issue costs. The new laws permit only 2 percent of proceeds of a bond issue to be applied toward issuance costs (excluding costs for credit enhancement). Costs of issuance are included in the 5 percent of net bond proceeds that may be applied toward "private activities." For issuers needing to bond these costs, offering additional bonds in the taxable markets is necessary. Under current Treasury regulations, taxable bonds issued to cover costs beyond the 2 percent limitation may be treated as separate issues despite their simultaneous offering with the tax-exempt issue.

Advance refundings. Qualified 501(c)3 bonds, but not other qualified private activity bonds, may be advance refunded. Such bonds issued after 1985 are only eligible for one advance refunding; bonds issued after 1986 may be advance refunded twice. Because of these limits, advance refundings may eventually be forced to be financed through the taxable markets.

High-to-low refundings in periods of significantly declining interest rates may still be profitable in the taxable markets. However, to achieve present value savings on the refunding of tax-exempt debt with taxable debt, taxable rates would have to fall significantly. This is unlikely in the near future. A more likely scenario may be the issuance of taxable advance refunding bonds to defease existing covenants or to restructure existing debt.

Tactical and Product Advantages of Taxable Debt

In evaluating financing alternatives, interest costs should be considered in conjunction with other expenses. For example, as administrative costs of compliance increase in response to the new regulations, the spread between tax-exempt and taxable debt may narrow. Under some circumstances, the inability to earn arbitrage profits or the necessity of using institutional funds to pay the costs of issuance may cause the total cost of tax-exempt debt to exceed the total cost of taxable funding.

Arbitrage restrictions. The new restrictions generally prohibit investing proceeds in obligations with materially higher yields (i.e., greater than one-eighth of 1 percent). With a few exceptions, all arbitrage earned on nonpurpose obligations must be rebated to the government. By issuing taxable debt, potential arbitrage opportunities are diminished because the spread between taxable borrowing costs and investment opportunities is narrow or negative. However, in periods of rising interest rates or if universities choose to invest in higher-risk/higher-yielding investments, reinvesting proceeds from taxable debt may afford investment opportunities equal to or greater than the interest costs of those bonds.

Reserve funds. Except for certain parity bonds, the new laws prohibit using more than 10 percent of the proceeds of tax-exempt debt to fund bond reserves. This will pose difficulties for institutions that for credit reasons need large amounts in reserves. Issuers may petition the IRS for a ruling permitting bonding for an amount greater than 10 percent. However, such rulings take time and in a period of rising interest rates the delay could be costly.

Pooled financings. If the proceeds of an issue are to be used for loans to two or more persons, the new laws impose time limitations on the investment of the proceeds. The maximum temporary period for which proceeds can be invested with un-restricted yields is now six months; it is 90 days for reinvestment of funds from loans either sold or repaid. Taxable domestic markets offer escape from these regulations. In addition, a pool of $100 million or more may be large enough to provide liquidity and lower overall costs.

Transition rule. Many universities received individual one-time transition rules on refunding rights. At least one university was granted special new money-issuing rights, up to a specified amount, on a one-time basis. On an interim basis it could be preferable to issue taxable debt until the aggregate financing required equals the allowable one-time financing amount.

Product advantages. The variety of products available through the taxable markets should enable higher education issuers to take advantage of market opportunities and to develop financing packages responsive to their long-term financial needs. Hedging products, such as interest rate swaps, currency swaps, caps, floors, and collars deserve special attention as they become more attractive to taxable debt issuers. For a detailed list and description of these various hedging products, see Richard E.

Anderson and Joel W. Meyerson, eds., *Financing Higher Education: Strategies After Tax Reform* (San Francisco: Jossey-Bass, 1987).

CASE STUDIES ON TAXABLE FINANCING IN THE DOMESTIC MARKET

The two following case studies of recent efforts by American universities to raise funds through the taxable markets illustrate the four considerations discussed above.

Cornell University

Cornell University recently required funding for the completion of the medical school's Lasdon Biomedical Center and the acquisition, renovation, and remodeling of the Alumni Center.

Legal constraints. Cornell's outstanding tax-exempt debt exceeded the $150 million volume cap imposed on private higher educational institutions by the Tax Reform Act of 1986. However, Cornell, a major research institution and land grant university, was granted a transition rule in the 1986 Tax Reform Act allowing it to borrow for qualified private activity purposes on a one-time basis up to an additional $150 million in the tax-exempt market.

The Alumni Center did not have a qualified private activity purpose, and therefore could not be financed on a tax-exempt basis. Although the medical school project qualified for tax-exempt funding, Cornell decided to preserve its $150 million transition rule and enter the taxable market.

Structural considerations. After exploring public and private taxable financing alternatives, Cornell decided to borrow through a private placement because of the available flexibility. Of particular importance to the university were call flexibility, an

93

amortizing structure with a long final maturity, and certain legal provisions (i.e., defeasance language). Call flexibility was desired to accommodate possible tax-exempt refinancing and to allow for retirement of debt with gifts when received. The amortizing structure was required to match debt service with anticipated cash flows from the financed projects. The legal provisions were essential in providing Cornell with maximum flexibility.

Outcome. Cornell wished to borrow on parity with its most recent $152.9 million borrowing through the Dormitory Authority of the State of New York. The private placement market was able to accommodate Cornell's requirements. Cornell University Revenue Bonds, 1987 Series A and B, were circled on October 6. These bonds were rated AA/Aa by Standard & Poor's and Moody's. The bonds are callable at a market price after a three-year no-call period. The 1987 Series A bonds have a final maturity of 2002, an average life of 9.5 years, and were priced at 110 basis points over the 10-year U.S. Treasury securities. The 1987 Series B bonds have a final maturity of 2012, an average life of 18 years, and were priced at 125 basis points over the interpolated 18-year U.S. Treasury securities. The primary security for this issue is the Pledged Revenues. Many secondary security features were stripped from this financing (i.e., no debt service fund or interim payments into a debt service fund).

Texas A&M University

Texas A&M University required funds to build a biotechnical research facility on the campus of the Houston Medical Center.

Legal constraints. Although Texas A&M is not constrained by the $150 million volume cap imposed on private universities and could fund the research project with tax-exempt bonds, three major factors pushed the university into the taxable market. Since the university was anticipating major donations for the facility, it was concerned about investment restrictions that would be placed on these donations if it borrowed on a tax-exempt basis. Because the new tax code does not permit more than 5 percent of the revenues from the research facility to be derived from nonprofit sources, the university was concerned about possible restrictions on its ability to lease space in the facility to for-profit entities. Finally, Texas A&M was concerned about yield restrictions on the Permanent University Fund, which is the ultimate security for the issue.

Structural considerations. The university wanted to structure the maturity of its issue to match expected receipts from fund raising. Although sufficient contributions were expected within three years, the university decided to finance the biotechnical center on a five year basis to give a margin for fund raising difficulties. Also, the university wanted to minimize the amount of negative arbitrage in the construction fund for the research facility.

Outcome. Because of the high credit quality, a competitive public offering was made. The issue had a five-year final maturity with no amortization of principal until the final year. This offering was very attractive to investors and, as a result, the university received 19 bids. The winning bid was only 41 basis points over the five-year Treasury note. Simultaneous with the bidding for this issue, the university bid out the investment of the construction fund. It received and accepted a bid for the construction fund that had an average life of only 2.5 years and was only 15 basis points lower than the borrowing cost.

___ THE GLOBAL TAXABLE MARKET

In today's global economy, one cannot speak of taxable domestic markets without considering the taxable markets worldwide. The trend toward globalization, including the development of multicurrency bonds and instruments to hedge against currency and interest rate fluctuations, enables both issuers and investors to access whatever markets meet their financial needs. Although closely linked, domestic and foreign markets are sufficiently distinct to warrant separate consideration. In general, the foreign markets have particular characteristics that may not be suited to all issuers. Some higher education issues may find that the size, speed, and demands on debt structure of foreign markets do not fit with their needs.

General Overview of Global Markets

Globalization of the capital markets allows capital to flow freely across national boundaries. In previous times, taxable markets were far less efficient because trading occurred around the world with few or no linkages between markets. The advent of 24-hour trading desks and rapid telecommunications systems has removed many inefficiencies, including discrepancies between exchange rates or the price of bonds. Of course, exchange rate arbitrage and inefficient pricing do occur at times, because, for example, the perceived risk of a bond issue may vary from market to market.

The rise of an assortment of dollar-denominated and foreign currency bonds allows financings to take advantage of international opportunities (such as currency fluctuations and interest rate differences) to achieve lower costs. The most common form of international debt is the Eurobond, which can be issued in dollars or in most major European or Asian currencies. The Eurobond is a debt instrument issued and traded in the international debt market outside the country of the borrower as well as outside the legal control of any specific country.

Eurobonds may be listed on several exchanges. However, there is no specific marketplace where they are traded. Many of the foreign markets also offer financing opportunities for issuers interested in borrowing in a currency and country other than their own. These bonds can be issued in any of several currencies, including the issuer's domestic currency. Samurai bonds, for example, can be American offerings issued in Japan in yen.

The internationalization of capital markets has promoted greater foreign investment in domestically offered issues. Both European and Japanese investors regularly purchase bonds in the U.S. domestic market. Concurrently, the U.S. Market has gained exposure to trends in the international economy and international capital flows. Concentration of foreign investors, such as the Japanese in the U.S. Treasury market, can cause an issue or issues (or even issuers) to become dependent on that particular foreign group of investors. If and when there is a change or shock in the foreign economy, the effect reverberates in the U.S. capital market.

There are two international markets of interest to the higher education issuer: the U.S. domestic market (with international investors' participation) and the international market abroad.

The International Market at Home

The domestic taxable markets offer issuers the opportunity to diversify their investor base while retaining flexibility in structuring their issues. The difference between interest rates and full costs of issuing debt in domestic taxable markets and in foreign markets depends on both the conditions of the markets and the degree of comfort each market has with the issue. Although the domestic market can attract foreign investors, it will not attract them in the same numbers as debt issued abroad. But the domestic markets are generally more comfortable with a variety of debt structures than are the foreign markets.

Taxable higher education bonds compete both domestically and internationally for the same investors targeted by other taxable issuers. It is also probable that taxable municipals will evolve in the domestic market as a hybrid of both taxable and tax-exempt markets. There have not been many taxable higher education issues; however, those transactions completed have been relatively well received. Although these slightly more complicated issues may have difficulty marketing themselves abroad, they may attract international investors domestically. In fact, foreign investor interest in these hybrids has already been dem-

97

onstrated. The Japanese were early and sizeable buyers of the Guaranteed Investment Contracts (GICs). A Japanese bank, Mitsui, also participated in a 1985 transaction with the Virginia Education Loan Authority, which will be examined later. As the market for higher education bonds grows in size and sophistication, participation by foreign investors should increase.

Higher education institutions must be prepared to accept higher direct costs, primarily because of the taxable nature of this type of debt. Having once decided to enter the taxable markets, costs may increase because of the novelty of higher education debt, the liquidity problems resulting from small issue size, and the additional costs of sales and other fees.

As with any new market, the early issues of higher education bonds are less efficiently priced. Investors expect to be compensated for unknowns. The average anticipated size of higher education issues (e.g., $75 million) is relatively small and will make them less liquid. The thin market and the absence of active trading makes the market for higher education bonds illiquid as investors are unable to convert their investments into cash as readily as in some other investment forms. This inability to remarket bonds requires a higher yield to investors. Given these constraints, issues are more difficult to sell so underwriting and sales fees will tend to be higher.

The International Market Abroad

Foreign markets may enable issuers to diversify and broaden their investor base, and thus increase the potential demand for future issues. Municipal issuers may attract investors who seek dollar-denominated bonds, but are nervous about corporate credits and stability. Dollar funding abroad may be available at a lower cost than it is domestically. As previously stated, issuers may profit from aberrations between markets caused by currency fluctuations or interest rate differentials.

Responsiveness to higher education bonds has not yet been tested abroad. The near-term outlook for issuing debt in foreign markets is not favorable because of size, maturity, and name recognition requirements. Typically, successful Eurobond issues require a minimum of $100 million for new issues. In addition, the markets look for short maturities (i.e., up to 10 years) with no call provisions or sinking fund or serial maturities. Name recognition is vital: the California system or Ivy League schools should meet this requirement, but most schools and agencies will not. Finally, foreign markets have recently turned conservative, with lowered tolerance for innovative or complicated financing.

These markets move extremely quickly. This can be problematic for universities and colleges accustomed to the slow pace of municipal markets. There are ways around some of the above limitations, but the effort can be costly.

"Roadshows" or obtaining credit enhancement, such as letters of credit from well-known, highly rated institutions, are two ways of overcoming lack of name recognition. Conducting roadshows involves a series of presentations to major investors in the relevant foreign markets. These meetings between investors and issuers may prove especially valuable for repeat financings. To augment investor awareness, institutions might (as Stanford has done) invite representatives to make on-sight visits to their campuses. But roadshows are costly. Securing letters of credit and other guarantees from recognized companies, banks, or agencies can also enhance the marketability of an issue, at a cost of 25 to 100 basis points on the issue. Despite their initial expense, these techniques may provide an overall lower all-in cost of financing.

Pooled financings may offer a viable alternative for individual users needing only limited amounts of capital. Pools of five or six universities each needing $20 million or less could take advantage of foreign market opportunities. However, such pools would likely be limited to "name" institutions, and even then might require a letter of credit. The final costs could still be too high to make deals economically viable. Of course, these and other costs may be offset by interest cost advantages in the foreign market.

A CASE STUDY ON THE INTERNATIONAL MARKET

The Virginia Education Loan Authority (VELA) was established in 1977 as a public authority of the Commonwealth of Virginia to increase access to postsecondary education through direct lending in the Stafford Loan Program. VELA remained a large supplemental direct lender until the early 1980s, when commercial banks increased their participation in student loan lending. Since then, VELA has decreased direct lending substantially in an effort to increase its role as a secondary market purchaser. It now provides liquidity to commercial banks who do not want to continue servicing student loans during the repayment period.

VELA's objective was to find alternative sources of affordable financing that comply with the Authority's conservative guidelines. The funds are used to originate or to purchase Stafford loans.

Legal Constraints

Since 1984 the U.S. Department of Education has severely curtailed tax-exempt student loan financing by subjecting issuers to a strict approval process and needs requirements. The Higher Education Act of 1986 moved the approval process to the state level. However, issuers are now subject to state tax-exempt volume caps and arbitrage restrictions.

Structural Considerations

The Authority has always entered into long-term financing agreements to match its funding with the maturities of its student loan portfolio. The Authority has tied the rate of interest on its funding sources to a Treasury Index, preferably the 3-month Bills, to match the quarterly Special Allowance Payments from the federal government. These payments are based on a quarterly average of 3-month Bills and provide eligible lenders like VELA with a guarantee yield on student loans.

Outcome

VELA has used financing techniques such as a taxable Japanese bank loan, and two taxable placements with the Student Loan Marketing Association (Sallie Mae). The first taxable transaction was an innovative $60 million loan from a Japanese bank in 1985. The loan was aggressively priced at 115 percent of 3-month Treasury Bills, and had a 2-year commitment period and a 10-year maturity. It was the first of its type placed with a Japanese lending institution. By the following year the Authority had already drawn all of the loan commitment, so it entered into a 5-year interim placement with Sallie Mae that was also priced as a percentage of 3-month Treasury Bills.

The most recent taxable transaction was a 15-year $180 million placement with Sallie Mae. Although VELA contemplated a number of alternatives, such as setting up a commercial paper program or issuing variable-rate demand bonds, the Sallie Mae placement offered the most aggressive pricing with the least risk. Sallie Mae also met the Authority's other requirements, such as Treasury-based pricing and long-term maturity. The transaction was structured to provide three separate interest rates that vary over time as a percentage of 3-month Treasury Bills. In addition, at any time during the 15-year life of the agreement VELA has the option to put to Sallie Mae any unamortized student loans purchased with proceeds of the payment. The $180 million is being used to pay off the outstanding Japanese bank loan and the recent 5-year transaction with Sallie Mae, and to provide $60 million to purchase new loans.

___ SUMMARY

The real impact of the Tax Reform Act of 1986 on higher education will be decided over time. But in the foreseeable future, higher education issuers will turn increasingly to offering taxable debt, either because they are barred from the tax-exempt market or because taxable markets offer advantages over the tax-exempt markets. Having once decided to issue taxable debt, higher education issuers may find that domestic private placement markets offer the greatest opportunities and flexibility for small issues. In the future, as higher education capital demands grow and that sector expands its use of techniques such as international pooled financings, European and Asian markets may become more accessible. In the immediate future, however, these markets may be less tolerant of small or relatively unknown higher education borrowers.

Until the taxable markets become more familiar with higher education issues, pricing may be less efficient for higher education borrowers than for corporate borrowers of comparable credit worthiness. The overall cost of issuing taxable debt will vary with the size and structure of the issue. However, the all-in costs of financing may be nearly equivalent when issuers consider savings on administrative and compliance costs, gains from arbitrage opportunities, and greater flexibility in debt structure. Use of products such as interest rate swaps, caps, and floors may further reduce the issuer's all-in cost of financing. The real cost differences will be elusive until the taxable market adjusts to higher education credits and higher education issuers adjust to the requirements for issuing taxable debt.

Of particular concern to higher education issuers in considering issuance of taxable debt is the implications of such an issuance for future credit ratings. Determining debt limitations will now involve considering the corporate market's emphasis on credit worthiness.

The most recent examples of taxable debt from higher education issuers show that these markets can offer attractive alternatives under certain conditions. Learning to recognize those conditions and select the strategy that best responds to the issuer's financial needs is one of the most critical tasks facing higher education administrators and financial officers.

7

CREDIT
ANALYSIS AND
ENHANCEMENT

DANIEL HEIMOWITZ

FAIR and uniform analysis of credit is particularly important in an international economy for several reasons. International competition has created economic pressures on the United States, one effect of which has been to increase domestic interest rates relative to the rates in foreign markets. Now that tax reform has limited the access of the largest private universities to tax-exempt markets, issuing taxable foreign debt has become an increasingly viable alternative for institutions with a high credit rating and name recognition.[1] In general, with more borrowers and lenders, uniform analysis of credit helps to insure a fair match between interest charged and credit risk. Although investment bankers can, and should, guide borrowers through the intricacies of credit ratings and credit enhancement, borrowers should have a knowledge of the basic principles used to assign credit risk and the techniques available to improve the rating of a debt issue.

1. David C. Clapp, "Tax Reform and the Bond Market," in *Financing Higher Education: Strategies After Tax Reform,* ed. Richard E. Anderson and Joel W. Meyerson (San Francisco: Jossey-Bass, 1987).

103

___ ESTABLISHING CREDIT RISK AND ___ RATINGS

One important point that many people unfamiliar with credit markets do not understand is that ratings apply to specific debt instruments, not directly to the borrowing institution. As a consequence, the pledges to each debt obligation are the starting point for rating. However, for obligations in which the college or university's credit is directly or indirectly pledged, the institution's general financial well-being is of paramount importance. In determining credit risk, the rating agencies will carefully examine demand for an institution's services, its income and expenditures, and its balance sheet.

Demand

The ability to repay debt is obviously dependent on a sufficient and stable revenue stream that, in turn, rests on a strong demand for the institution's services. Most colleges and universities are primarily dependent on tuition income or enrollment-driven state support. Student demand is, therefore, a key factor in establishing credit risk. Obviously, the number of students enrolling is important, but applications, acceptance rates, student quality, and the nature and level of the competition are also carefully assessed. Undergirding the demand for an institution's services are the quality of the faculty and programs and general institutional reputation, which is also evaluated.

Similarly, if research and service revenue are important as sources of support, credit agencies must determine the stability and level of demand for them as well. Again, quality of faculty and programs is considered as well as trends in research and service support.

Revenue and Expenditures

An institution's revenues and expenditures are evaluated for level and stability. And, obviously, they should balance. Diversity of support is also important. For example, in a recent review of college and university financial ratings that was undertaken in support of the U.S. Department of Education's sale of College Housing and Academic Facilities Loan Program loans, it was determined that tuition represented only 25 percent of revenues at colleges with *Aaa*- and *Aa*- rated debt. But at colleges with *Baa*- and *Ba*- rated debt, it represented 70.1 percent. This discrepancy is not, as it turns out, simply a proxy for public- or private-sector support. The higher-rated group had an average 1986 tuition of $11,340 compared to $6,132 for the lower-rated group. Debt service coverage, measured by dividing annual debt service payments into current fund revenue, is another critical indicator of credit worthiness taken from current fund revenues and expenditures.

Balance Sheet

In the analysis of credit risk, credit agencies carefully review an institution's balance sheet. The full range of assets and debt is reviewed. Quality and availability of the assets must be determined; then the level of debt and the pledges of the existing debt on institutional assets and revenue streams will be reviewed. Three significant ratios are:

- Expendable fund balances to plant debt.
- Plant equity to plant debt.
- Currently available assets to short-term liabilities.

Acceptable and desirable ratios will vary by institutional type and sector.

Financial performance and balance sheet strength are closely analyzed. Although no one factor is critical and each

105

institution is individually evaluated, institutional and academic strengths are usually reflected in key financial ratios. Endowment per student, prior to the October 19, 1987, stock market slide, was $69,000 for the *Aaa* and *Aa* group and $1,800 for the *Baa* and *Ba* group. For the higher-rated group, debt was 29 percent of endowment, compared to 289 percent for the lower-rated group.

Public Colleges and Universities

When evaluating debt issued by a public college or university, the rating agencies must consider the underlying economic condition of the government that supports the debt. This is obviously the determining factor for a general obligation bond but it is important for revenue bonds as well. If the state or local government is in a strong financial condition, it will be able to support the institution directly, which in turn will be able to meet its debt obligations.

Outside Credit Support—Substitution and Enhancement

Credit support for college and university financing is used for a variety of reasons, as varied as the borrowing requirements and financial wherewithal of America's higher educational institutions. Available support mechanisms change the borrower's debt obligation, creating a debt instrument with different credit and investment characteristics than the borrower could achieve directly. The techniques are often used by weaker or unknown borrowers to gain a more favorable interest rate. Stronger issuers use them to maximize the benefit of their strengths or as an alternative to obligating their total resources. They may be used to support long-term borrowings or borrowings for financial purposes on a short-term, variable rate basis.

Outside credit support improves the credit quality of an issue, simplifies for investors an otherwise complex security arrangement, or could be used to support some portion of a financing for which the issuer's resources may be inadequate. The outside support may totally substitute for the issuer's credit or it may just provide a necessary enhancement to the basic security provided by the issuer.

If the issuer has outstanding debt without credit substitution, the other ratings of the borrower are reviewed in light of a new issue *with* credit substitution. If no other debt is outstanding, general credit assessment of the borrower is still undertaken so that the credit implications of the issue for the financial guarantor or insurer can be determined.

Credit Substitution

Credit agencies recognize a substitution for an issuer's credit when a rated bank or rated insurance company is legally bound, under all circumstances, to pay all principal and interest when due. When credit substitution is used, the credit agency must evaluate the ability of the substituting entity to fulfill its obligation. For college and university financing, the two most commonly used forms of credit substitution are bank letters-of-credit and bond insurance.

Letters-of-credit. The ratings of bonds and notes secured with letters-of-credit take into consideration the bank issuing the letter and the support mechanism. If the letter-of-credit support mechanism clearly substitutes the bank's financial strength for the borrower's, then the bonds are rated at the same level as the bank's senior obligations. To ensure that all potential problems are foreseen, credit agencies assume that the issuer of the letter-of-credit–backed debt will default on its repayment of obligations and file for bankruptcy. This is, of course, for analytical purposes only.

There are three generic types of letters-of-credit used to back debt instruments. Each is designed to achieve certain objectives and results in a particular legal structure. The three types are: direct pay, standby (warehousing), and standby (clawback). Al-

107

though the ratings do not distinguish among these types of structure, the analysis for each is quite different.

In a *direct pay* structure, the letter-of-credit is used for all normal payments of principal and interest on the debt, whether at maturity, at special or mandatory redemption. Or at acceleration.

In a *standby (warehousing)* structure, the letter-of-credit is used, in combination with other funds, to pay debt service or purchase nonremarketed tendered bonds. The other funds, typically issuer or borrower debt repayments, are held by the bond trustee for a sufficient time before payment to bondholders to ensure that payments are not subject to recoupment from bondholders in the event of issuer or borrower bankruptcy.

In a *standby (clawback)* structure, the letter-of-credit normally is used only if there are insufficient funds to pay debt service, including funds subject to attack as preferences.

To obtain credit substitution for letter-of-credit–backed debt, regardless of the type of letter-of-credit used, five areas must be examined: enforceability, sufficiency, duration, mechanics, and preference.

The most straightforward analytic task is to ensure that the letter-of-credit is irrevocable and is the legal, valid, and binding obligation of the bank. The letter-of-credit must be legally issued, in conformity with both general and specific internal bank requirements.

Once the letter-of-credit is determined to be the bank's legal obligation, the next step is to determine whether it is sufficient to cover the entire amount of the debt. As a general standard, the letter-of-credit must cover full principal of the debt issue plus sufficient interest to pay accrued interest through any call date (at the maximum rate permitted on the debt if the debt is variable rate), plus a contingency provision equal to five days of interest at the maximum rate.

Credit rating agencies examine the structure of the transaction to ensure that the letter-of-credit will, in fact, be in force and available for drawing when required. If the letter-of-credit expires after final bond maturity, Moody's requires that there be (at minimum) a five-day time-lag bond maturity and expiration of the letter. If the letter-of-credit expires before the bond's final maturity, the bond issue must be redeemed or tendered at least five days before the letter-of-credit's expiration.

The mechanics of the structure are examined to ensure the timely payment of principal premiums (if any), interest, and purchase price. It is necessary to trace the flow of funds of the transaction through all payments to bondholders in order to ensure that all debt service (and, with a demand bond, the purchase price) will be made when due. Therefore, the instructions to the trustee for drawing upon the letter-of-credit in a timely fashion to pay bondholders must be clear and direct.

To avoid payment defaults, the timing of all notices and actions in the indenture or resolution must coincide with the timing provisions of the letter-of-credit or liquidity support documents. Under the U.S. Bankruptcy Code, payments made by a bankrupt organization from its own property in repayment of its preexisting debt obligations within 90 days before the filing of the bankruptcy petition may be recovered (recouped), under certain circumstances, by a bankruptcy trustee or debtor-in-possession from the recipients of such payments (preferential payments or avoidable preferences). Such preferential payments will be replaced in the estate of the bankrupt and redistributed to the bankrupt's creditors in accordance with the bankruptcy liquidation or reorganization plan.

Bond insurance. In contrast to letter-of-credit–backed bonds, municipal bond insurance programs provide uniform coverage under a standard policy. A municipal bond insurance policy is a noncancellable guarantee, designed to protect the bondholder from nonpayment by the issuer. With few exceptions, when an issuer fails to meet a scheduled principal or interest payment, the insurer must make the debt service payment on the issuer's behalf in a full and timely manner.

A brief note on the credit evaluation of municipal bond insurance companies is relevant. Municipal bond insurance companies like AMBAC Indemnity Corporation, Bond Investors Guaranty, Financial Guaranty Insurance Company, Financial Security Assurance, Inc., and Municipal Bond Investors Assurance Corporation obviously protect their credit rating with great care. Their rating is based on a number of factors, including the aggregate quality of the bonds they insure, the volume of their business, and the insurance company's assets and cash flow. One thing that issuers should recognize is that aggregate quality of the portfolio is determined, in part, by the diversification of the portfolio (i.e., type of bonds issued and geographical and industry dispersion of issuers). Consequently, issues (and issuers) may vary in attractiveness to insurance companies.

Credit Enhancement

Issuers are now utilizing support for their financing transactions in forms less binding than irrevocable letters-of-credit, bond insurance, or full collateralization. Issuers often seek outside bank support to bolster *some portion of a transaction* rather than have a bank assume the entire credit risk. In these cases, credit rating agencies do not view the bank's credit as a substitution for the issuer's credit. Rather, the bank's role is just one necessary support that enhances the basic credit offered by the issuer.

Standby liquidity. Standby liquidity for demand bonds and commercial paper programs is frequently offered if the issuer's resources are inadequate or refinancing proceeds are unavailable. Both the frequency with which liquidity might be needed and the magnitude of the potential obligation relative to the strengths of the issuer are considered when evaluating the quality and likely availability of the standby liquidity. Similarly, note and bond purchase agreements are sometimes offered in support of bond anticipation notes or bonds with balloon maturities, particularly where the issuer has little or no demonstrated market success. These purchase agreements assure investors that they will be paid at maturity even if the issuer does not have sufficient funds on hand and for any reason cannot gain market access for refinancing.

110

Collateralization. Credit enhancement can be achieved by pledging high quality and appropriately liquid investments in support of the debt. Sometimes collateral arrangements let the issuer be its own source of alternative liquidity for variable rate debt. There are many concerns regarding the quality, adequacy, and expected availability of collateral offered either as a primary source of security or as a source of alternative liquidity. A legal opinion affirming the collateral's availability to bondholders is important, especially when the source of the collateral is an endowment that may be subject to prior restrictions. To cover future collateral shortfalls resulting from market or investment losses, we look at the borrower's plans and capabilities for replenishment of collateral. In the case of variable rate debt, an important security feature is a provision for full debt retirement through a mandatory tender prior to an event of collateral insufficiency. If the collateral is of sufficiently high quality and the mechanisms are workable, credit agencies look to the underlying collateral as one source for bondholder payments.

The collateralization of a bond issue with a portfolio of investments is a credit enhancement that has been used by many colleges and universities. Typically, colleges and universities have issued bonds secured by a general or revenue pledge and have additionally pledged a portion of their unrestricted endowment as security. The availability of unrestricted endowment has enabled colleges to collateralize their bond issues and, in doing so, achieve an improved credit rating and lower interest costs. Although this double layer of protection can enhance the quality of the particular issue, the level of enhancement depends on the restrictions governing the quality and maintenance of the collateral and on the general credit strength of the university.

In analyzing a collateralized bond issue, the level of credit enhancement must take into account the likelihood of the collateral's being available to support the bond issue if for any reason the pledged revenues are unavailable. Therefore, the collateral must, first, be readily marketable; real property and other tangible investments are generally unsuitable. Most collateralized issues limit investments of collateral to rated debt issues and U.S. Government and agency debt. Publicly traded equities are sometimes included, but their relative volatility makes them poorly suited for collateralization. Once collateral is established, the pledged collateral must be regularly valued based on current market conditions. Valuations should be conducted by independent parties, and the frequency of valuation should be specified in the bond indenture. The bond documents must also define the time period in which any collateral shortfall must be cured.

Required collateral level, frequency of collateral valuation, and requirements for collateral replenishment are closely related. The collateral level should be equal to the par value of bonds outstanding plus some additional level of coverage. The longer the period between valuations and the greater the lag between valuation and replenishment, the larger the potential market loss in collateral value. Therefore, the more frequently the collateral is valued and the more frequently it is replenished, the lower the additional level of collateral required.

Collateralization is considered a means of credit enhancement, rather than credit substitution, because the source of collateral replenishment is the borrower's own resources. If an institution is in a weak financial condition and had a low level of unrestricted endowment in excess of that which is initially used to collateralize a bond issue, and if market declines reduce collateral value, other endowment losses will further weaken the institution's ability to replenish collateral levels. Conversely, where a college has a large endowment and is generally strong financially, it should be able to meet any required replenishment.

Securitization. Securitization is a means of pooling financial assets, such as mortgages or receivables, where the purchased assets provide the essential security for the debt issue. A debt issue will be securitized by a pool of assets if the asset pool's par value is larger than the debt issue, and if its expected revenue generation is greater than the debt issue's debt service requirements. This extra collateralization is generally considered necessary to compensate for potential losses in future asset value. Financing of receivables, such as student loans, or pooling the debt of many issuers (as was done in the 1987 federal asset sale of college housing and academic facility loans by the U.S. De-

112

partment of Education), are ways in which securitization can allow a debt issue to be well secured by assets that are individually of a lower credit quality. Performance data is necessary to develop a profile of prospective losses for each type of securitized asset, which is in turn used to set the required levels of over-securitization.

SUMMARY

In today's environment of limited public support for capital projects, more colleges and universities are turning to the credit markets to finance equipment and construction. To participate effectively, institutional leaders should have a reasonably detailed understanding of credit market mechanisms. This chapter briefly reviewed credit evaluation and considered some of the mechanisms available to institutions to improve the ratings of bonds they issue.

If a college or university's general credit is pledged, the bond's rating will be heavily influenced by the basic institutional financial and strategic strengths. For most institutions, strong enrollment demand is critical. A diverse income base is important, as is a sound balance sheet. Institutions may improve the rating of any specific issue with credit support. This support may substitute for the institution's credit or simply enhance it.

8

MORTGAGE-
BACKED
STUDENT
LOANS

DOUGLAS WOFFORD

WITH the rising costs of a college education and a flattening enrollment base, higher education officials have begun to reconceptualize the options available for financing a college education. In particular, some college officials have challenged the long-held notion that, when it comes to money, an institution's principal interaction with a family should be in the financial aid office. Instead, a new concept is emerging suggesting that colleges and state financing organizations must go beyond passive involvement or simple needs analysis. In short, some colleges are determining that higher education must reconsider its role in the financial packaging of its product.

Taking the lead from private enterprise, more colleges now understand that the *form* of finance can be almost as important as a net price. For example, cars are "sold" on the basis of how well a monthly payment will fit into a family's budget. Yet when it comes to financing a college education, institutions have traditionally stressed the often-threatening net price, without supporting that price with manageable payment options.

Recognizing that families with college-age children were facing a growing financial burden, a few colleges and universities in the early 1980s began developing financing packages that extended beyond the basic needs analysis. Other institutions have followed suit, directing their "packaging" efforts primarily at middle- and upper-middle-income families. Loan arrangements have become the centerpiece of the financing; there is, after all, only so much grant aid available. In addition, attempts have been made to increase the value of these programs by handling the application process at the institution, a form of "one-stop shopping."

Most notable in this effort has been the University of Pennsylvania, where the "Penn Plan" has, since 1984, offered an ever-increasing "menu" of financing options, including guaranteed tuition through single or extended payments, long-term financing for nonaided students, and a revolving line of credit for general educational expenses.

For those that itemized deductions, the cost of this debt financing was eased by the fact that interest charges could be deducted from their taxable income. For many families the after-tax cost of borrowing may have been only half of the interest charged. Consequently, this new form of financial packaging was not only convenient, but could be relatively inexpensive.

The Tax Reform Act of 1986 and the Omnibus Budget Reconciliation Act of 1987 made sweeping revisions of the nation's tax laws. Among the changes was the provision that consumer interest charges could no longer be used to reduce taxable income. As a result, the net expense to borrowers of some of the recently developed financing packages increased dramatically. Congress did, however, leave one type of borrowing with deductible interest in the revised tax code—mortgages on a first or second home.

In effect, the new law has created obstacles and special opportunities for higher education. The significance of this dual challenge and opportunity is underscored by the fact that the net cost of federal student loans—Stafford loans and particularly the Parent Loans for Undergraduate Students (PLUS) that were intended for middle-income parents—has been increased with the new nondeductibility provision. On the other hand, the opportunity exists for colleges, universities, and state agencies to retain some of the prior tax advantages of their loan programs by creating mortgage-backed student loans.

THE TAX CODE AND QUALIFIED
INTEREST DEDUCTIBILITY

Although consumer interest deductions will be completely phased out by 1991, "qualified residence interest," as defined by section 163 (H) of the income tax code, shall continue to be tax deductible. One key requirement is that the indebtedness must be secured by the taxpayer's property. At the time interest is paid or accrued, the property must be a "qualified residence" of the taxpayer.

A "qualified residence" can include both the principal residence of the taxpayer and one other residence owned by the taxpayer. There are, however, restrictions in the definition of a second residence. A second residence shall be considered "qualified" if it meets one of the following two criteria:

1. The residence is used by the taxpayer for personal purposes for a number of days that exceeds the greater of 14 days, or 10 percent of the number of days during the year that the residence is rented at a fair rental.
2. The taxpayer does not use or rent the residence at any time during a taxable year.

The law allows full interest on debt that is secured by a residence when the money is used to buy, build, or substantially improve a home. A restriction that has been added, however, is a $1 million limit on such interest-deductible debt.

Different rules apply, however, for any interest deduction on home-equity borrowing—debt secured by a residence and used for something other than buying, building, or improving the home. The law limits interest deductions on home-equity borrowing to debt not exceeding the fair market value of the residence less the acquisition indebtedness of the home or $100,000, whichever is less. The home-equity loan can, though, be used for any purpose, including education.

For the amount of a home-equity loan that exceeds the limitations, the interest is deductible only if the money is used for home improvements. Home-equity debt that does not qualify as residence indebtedness is treated as personal debt for which interest deductions began to be phased out in 1987.

Homeowners who want to refinance an existing mortgage will find the law limiting. A refinancing is treated like a home-equity loan, although the balance of the prior mortgage is not counted against the $100,000 limit. Thus, someone with a $40,000 mortgage balance on a home whose fair market value is $300,000 would have $260,000 of equity, but can fully deduct interest on a refinancing of only $140,000—the $40,000 mortgage balance, plus the $100,000 ceiling on home-equity debt.

The changes also penalize homeowners who made large down payments on their homes. If someone bought a $350,000 home with a $175,000 down payment and a $175,000 mortgage, the interest deduction is limited to that on $100,000 of additional debt, unless the money is used for home improvements.

The bottom line, however, is that mortgage-backed loans still remain the only loans for which the interest may be 100 percent deductible. For many middle-income families, the home may be the largest asset they have to borrow against to finance education.

___ INSTITUTIONAL POLICY
___ CONSIDERATIONS

The new tax law offers special opportunities for colleges and state agencies to establish mortgage-backed student loans. However, the private financial sector will certainly step in and provide appropriate products. Why should colleges and agencies consider their own programs? The answers are: (1) it is a valuable service for families; (2) colleges and universities are, in some respects, in a better position to offer the service than the private financial sector; and (3) the programs can provide institutions with a competitive advantage relative to other institutions.

The "valuable service" response is especially relevant to state loan authorities. Their purpose is to provide effective financing for higher education. For many families in the current tax environment, this cannot be achieved without mortgage-backed debt.

Institutions, too, are motivated by the service issue, but there are also reasons why they can provide the financing more effectively than private financial institutions. Colleges and universities might charge lower interest rates, or guarantee the debt to a bank, which would enable the bank to charge lower interest rates. A commercial lender has no particular interest in establishing the loan except for the interest it receives. The institution clearly has more at stake. The use of family debt financing may even reduce college financial aid expenditures. Moreover, the college has a more involved relationship with the student. If the college does its job well, a positive bond will be formed with the student. These factors may reduce the credit risk to the institution and, therefore, the interest it must charge as compensation for risk.

Finally, if colleges want to provide comprehensive financing at competitive rates, they must use mortgage-backed loans. For some families the decision to select one institution over another may be determined, in part, by the convenience of fitting payments into the family budget without having to arrange financing through their own bank—in other words, one-stop financial shopping.

If an institution decides that the costs and administration are not too burdensome and that there may be advantages to creating a mortgage-backed program, it should ask itself the following questions:

1. Who are our clientele?   In considering the clientele for the mortgage-backed program, you can easily narrow down the field to those families who own a home. However, of those: Will our students and families avail themselves of the program? Are they using debt now? What tax bracket are they in? Do they itemize? (Experts predict that only about 30 percent of taxpayers will itemize under the new law.) Although the more financially sophisticated parents may be quicker to perceive the value of the loan program, they are also more capable of arranging mortgage financing on their own. Less sophisticated parents may not understand the financial advantages but they may be attracted by the convenience of protracted payment.

2. What is our niche in the market?   As more institutions offer the financial convenience of the mortgage-backed loans, there will be increasing pressure on other colleges and universities to follow suit. But each institution must look not just at the competitive marketplace, but at its own mission to serve students and families.

3. Can this financial option help further institutional goals, not only numeric enrollment goals but also goals of access and diversity?   Like any financial option, the mortgage-backed program should be considered part of a broader philosophical approach to college financing—not just as a way to keep up with the other college Joneses. It is possible, for example, that by offering financing alternatives to middle- and upper-income families, an institution can increase unrestricted funds for lower-income families. With such an outcome, the institution is able to broaden the access to higher education by packaging appropriate financial aid options for different income levels. That's a mission approach—not a competitive one.

4. What expertise can we bring to bear on the implementation of a mortgage-backed program? In analyzing whether or not to proceed with a mortgage-backed option, an institution should consider its ability to launch such a sophisticated program. Does the institution have the talent within its ranks to carry out such a program? Can it recruit the help needed? Or can the institution wait until title companies and attorneys begin to offer their services to help the institution develop the desired program?

5. Does the college have the financial resources or is there a bank that would provide the necessary financing? Establishing a loan program requires a commitment of resources from the institution, from a cooperative bank, or quite possibly from both. The college must carefully examine the impact of any commitments on its operation budget, endowment fund, or both.

Summary. What it all comes down to is that the mortgage-backed option is more than just an exciting new trend created by the Tax Reform Act. Instead, this new option must be examined in the light of an institution's mission, its constituency, and its resources.

___ PRACTICAL CONSIDERATIONS

Although changes in the tax law seem to make mortgage-based lending a desirable option, colleges and agencies must consider several practical issues concerning administrative and logistical problems before embarking on such a program.

The mortgage. Central to a mortgage-based loan program is the idea that an institution would hold a family's mortgage as security on the loan. Because of this, college lenders must understand the role of the mortgage as a legal instrument.

In a home purchase, the mortgage is not the loan—or the note—itself. Instead, it is a piece of paper that stays in the background as long as the borrower continues to pay on the loan. The mortgage only becomes an issue if the borrower does not pay. In that instance, it spells out the rights of the lender in recovering the proceeds of the loan from the property.

The National Conference on Uniform State Laws defines a mortgage as "any form of instrument whereby title to real estate is reserved or conveyed as security for the payment of a debt or other obligation." The first step for the lender, then, is to determine if the mortgage security interest meets the following legal requirements. Note that these are "typical" requirements; actual requirements vary from state to state.

1. The mortgage must be a written instrument. Oral agreements can be formal contracts, but they hold no power in agreements affecting real property.
2. It must commit the borrower to pay the lender a specific sum under specific terms. The terms of the formal contract, including the amount to be repaid and the repayment schedule, must be spelled out.
3. There must be a default clause allowing the holder of the note to proceed against the borrower personally for a breach of obligations under the terms of the note, as well as for a breach of the mortgage covenants. This points out that the note and the mortgage are two different instruments.
4. The note must be properly executed and voluntarily delivered and accepted.
5. The parties must have contractual capacity.

Minimum requirements. If a college plans to hold a mortgage as a security, it should check to see that the note, at a minimum, includes the following: (1) appropriate identification of the mortgagor and the mortgagee; (2) proper description of the property that is liened; (3) covenants of seizin and warranty (the state of owning the property being conveyed); and (4) provision for release of dower (the interest in a husband's real estate given by law to the widow for support after his death) by the mortgagor.

Appraisal.   Although not absolutely required, many lenders ask for a recent appraisal of the property value (even for a second or third mortgage). Opinion is split on whether a home appraisal should be required in an educational loan program, especially since the cost of an appraisal can be a burden for the family. Because it is not required legally, some institutions have opted to eliminate the appraisal to save the family money. Others, however, do require the appraisal because it is standard procedure and protects the lender.

Verification and recording.   Mortgage lenders generally verify the title and have the mortgage duly recorded into the public record in the local county or township. Typically, this requires the involvement of a national title company, since a college or university usually will not be ready to establish a national network of representatives to carry out title searches and mortgage recording. Crucial to a successfully administered mortgage-backed loan option, then, is an institution's trusted relationship with a reputable title company.

Summary.   The special requirements of a mortgage routinely extend the length of time required to approve a loan after application has been made. A six- to eight-week turnaround should be expected. In addition, a mortgage option increases the costs of the loan, through recording fees, closing costs, and special state and local taxes and fees. Those costs must either be absorbed by the loan program or be explained and passed on to the family.

Fulfilling the minimum requirements of establishing a mortgage obligation is not very onerous, although the additional steps of appraising, verifying, and recording do require more effort and resources. There are reasons in addition to debt security, however, for colleges to wish to go beyond the minimum requirements.

___ PUBLIC POLICY ISSUES

Before undertaking mortgage-backed student loans, higher education must fully consider the impact of these programs on public perception and policy in the following four areas:

1. Might higher education appear to be abusing the tax law for self-serving reasons?
2. Are colleges and universities competing unfairly with the commercial sector?
3. Are the plans fair to students and families?
4. Is it good policy to remove students formally from the debt agreement?

There has been some indication that Congress has begun to view higher education as just another special-interest group, protecting its own turf at the expense of others. If, then, a number of colleges, universities, and agencies become involved in mortgage-backed loan programs, and if some of these programs adhere to only the minimum legal requirements, the overall effect may be to reinforce the special-interest-group image.

On the other hand, it can be argued that by offering mortgage-backed loans, colleges are simply taking fair advantage of a specific opportunity written into the tax code by Congress. If that opportunity exists in order to improve middle-class families' access to higher education, then the more widely these loans are available, the more the public interest will be served.

Colleges and agencies must carefully consider how their mortgage-backed loan programs will be perceived, paying attention to both substance and form. Substantively, how do higher education programs compare with commercial ones? Is there more to the mortgage backing than interest deductibility? For example, if a family pledges property in support of a loan, will they pay a lower interest rate or receive some other form of consideration? In form, how is the program marketed? Do any materials describing the program make it sound like an abuse of the tax code?

From another angle, small businesses have argued that non-profit organizations—colleges and universities in particular—are competing unfairly with business in areas that are not central to their mission. The sale of computers, clothing, non-textbooks, records, and tapes have all been called into question. In fact, higher education has not been well received when it has attempted to defend these activities before a Congressional committee.

The question, then, must be asked: Should higher education be in the lending business at all? In the case of mortgage-backed lending, it can be argued that the program serves students by making financing more convenient. But is this enough? The question may be moot, if it can be shown that commercial banking is not interested in the segment of the educational marketplace served by mortgage-backed loans. In the meantime, institutions may be able to sidestep the issue by forging an alliance with a local bank (if a willing partner is available) and combining the expertise of both groups.

Is it reasonable for families to undertake the debt of a mortgage-backed loan? In light of growing public concern over personal indebtedness, colleges and universities must carefully consider the situation of each family. If the actual cost is unreasonable for a particular family, the possibility of a tax advantage should not be exploited; it could be disastrous to higher education if a legislator were to point out how a "greedy" college encouraged a family to borrow and then foreclosed. This situation calls for even more careful consideration if an institution draws students from a limited geographic area in which, if the economy declines, the college may be crushed between its financial needs and external political pressures.

Finally, mortgage-backed debt may tend to institutionalize the "debt shift" from child to parent. In the past, loan instruments generally were in the name of the student (although some packages required a parental comaker). In mortgage-backed debt, however, parents will be more involved. Is it good public policy to distance the student from any legal responsibility for the debt? Conversely, is it wise for parents to trust their financial security to the faithfulness of their children?

There are no clear answers to these public policy issues. The current legislative climate calls for caution on the part of higher education, which would do well to explore the problems openly with members of Congress and the Treasury. By addressing the issues directly and, perhaps, setting self-imposed guidelines, higher education may be able to continue to take advantage of this valuable provision of the tax code.

IMPLEMENTATION OF THE MORTGAGE-BACKED PROGRAM: TWO TYPES OF PLANS

To date, only a handful of institutions and states have completed the extensive research and planning necessary to introduce mortgage-backed programs. Fewer yet have actually begun offering mortgage-backed loans.

The University of Pennsylvania and the Massachusetts Education Loan Authority (MELA) have both implemented mortgage-backed options, exemplifying two of the types of programs that may become prototypes.

These two programs differ in that, for the Penn Plan, the university starts the loan process by working with families, then works with a bank and title company for administration of the program. The proceeds of the loan can only be used at the University of Pennsylvania. MELA, on the other hand, is a state loan authority that works with a large number of institutions within the state of Massachusetts. The MELA program buys loans from universities and then offers the borrowers the option of securing their loans with a second mortgage.

The following profiles of the two programs include the philosophies and administrative considerations of implementing the mortgage-backed option.

The Penn Plan: Initiated by the University

Penn's mortgage-backed lending can only be understood in the context of the wider Penn Plan, of which secured loans are only a small part. Instituted in 1983, the Penn Plan was set up to meet the needs of families who were not eligible for aid and didn't know that financing options were available.

The Penn Plan offers families a wide menu of financing options, including guaranteed tuition prepayment in which a family either pays out of their own funds or takes out a loan for the prepayment. Revolving lines of credit are available in different versions. And there is a monthly budgeting plan that allows a family to extend payments.

The mortgage-backed option, then, is another wrinkle in an already extensive program. Tied to the prepayment plan, it allows families to secure their prepayment loan with a mortgage, protecting their interest deductibility.

In setting up the program, Penn drew on its established working relationship with Philadelphia National Bank (PNB). By negotiating with the bank and with Commonwealth Land Title Company (and with PNB and one of the divisions of Commonwealth negotiating the work flow and the charges involved), Penn was able to work out a plan in which the university would do the initial counseling of families interested in the plan. But once the application was filled out, the bank and title company would actually process the loan.

Unlike other Penn Plan loans, which are typically processed in about four weeks time, the mortgage-backed loans often take up to eight weeks, with applications cycling from PNB to Commonwealth, the attorneys, the family, then back through Commonwealth and PNB.

As a result of the extra time required, Penn realized that students' accounts might not be credited in time for the August draw-downs. This meant changing policy and putting temporary credits on the accounts of students who had been approved for the loans, so that the students could still register without worry of late fees.

The decision to secure a loan is the family's, but Penn Plan counselors work with the student and family to make sure they understand all the ramifications of the option, and that they talk with their own tax advisor. Penn recommends that parents opt for a prepayment plan—either secured or nonsecured—only when the student plans to spend four years at the university, without transferring, without becoming aided after a year or two (if a sibling also enrolled at Penn, for instance), and without spending time overseas on a program not affiliated with Penn.

After Penn has screened the applicant, the application goes to PNB for a credit check and, for a mortgage-backed loan, a copy of the deed. If the credit is good, PNB will begin working with the title company to do the title search and recording. All papers are prepared by the bank (which designed all new forms, a new agreement, and a new disclosure for the program), bundled with the university's agreements, and sent to the family.

For the monthly draw-downs of the funds, money is wired from PNB to the university. Penn pays the bursar's office the amount due, and the remainder is invested.

The program is offered both to new participants in the guaranteed tuition program and to former participants who have been given the option of refinancing. To date, about one-third of all new loan applicants have opted for the secured loans. And of those students applying only for the prepayment program, half are taking out second-mortgage loans.

Based on their experience, Penn Plan officials offer the following points to consider in setting up such a program.

1. *Build in plenty of lead time.* The Penn Plan already had an extensive loan program in place, with the staff, legal counsel, computer system, and institutional support to make it work. Adding the mortgage-backed program was just like adding another item to the menu. Even so, the short time allotted to implement the program taxed the facilities and staff. Colleges should expect to spend about nine months on the implementation.

2. *Be prepared for questions.* With a new program, the public will be interested and inquisitive. A close working relationship between institution and bank can help ease the burden of questions from families.

3. *Develop a comfortable working relationship with the attorneys.*

4. *Become well-versed in state statutes regarding second mortgages.* Texas is the only state in which Penn's mortgage-backed program is not offered, because the Texas constitution offers homestead protection and disallows second mortgages. Research on such issues is now available through sources such as MELA, but it should be reviewed by each institution.

5. *Determine the institution's day-to-day involvement with administration of the program.* In Penn's case, the decision was "not at all." "This means that, when a family calls the Penn Plan and asks about the status of their application, they are referred to the bank.

6. *Install a computer system that can interface with different areas of the university.* Allow plenty of time, too, for installation and programming.

7. *Draw on as many contacts as possible for advice and ideas.* Solicit information from families, alumni, donors, and other members of the campus community.

8. *Consider the publications that will be needed to communicate the structure of the program.*

9. *Consider the amount of money that will be required up front.* Because the Penn Plan had already established a mutual level of trust with PNB, it was able to enter into the mortgage-backed program without a great deal of up-front money. Smaller colleges, and those institutions without such a relationship, might be expected to provide higher collateral or guarantees.

10. *Solicit help from all areas of the college.* The Penn Plan was designed using a cross-disciplinary approach, pulling in people from all branches of the university for weekly meetings to hash out the concept and the design. This, in effect, allowed the Penn Plan to win the support of the entire college

11. *Make sure the title company is large enough to serve the anticipated needs.* Because the secured loan program requires the recording of a title in a student's state of residence, the title company must be able to send representatives to each state.

12. *Work out a flexible arrangement with the bank.* Thanks to the trust built up between Penn and PNB, the bank is flexible in

accommodating unexpected situations—such as twins who both attend the university and are both covered under one home mortgage.

13. *Establish a policy on what to do in case of a foreclosure.* In Penn's case, PNB agreed to offer the same interest rate on both secured and nonsecured loans, indicating that they didn't anticipate foreclosing on anyone's home.

14. *Consider the quality of the loan portfolio, no matter what the size of the school.* Even small schools can build strong relationships with banks, based on the fact that the loans will be made to families who don't qualify for aid, meaning that they have significant income and are generally good credit risks.

MELA: A Plan Authorized By the State

Concerned about the widening gap between the cost of education and the ability of families to pay, the legislature of the Commonwealth of Massachusetts in 1982 created the Massachusetts Education Loan Authority (MELA). Established to provide supplemental loan programs, MELA began lending money in the spring of 1983, with nine institutions within Massachusetts involved the first year.

MELA's board, appointed by the governor, is comprised of educators and members of the financial and banking community. The state's secretary of economic affairs is an ex officio member.

The money is loaned through two separate programs: the Family Education Loan (FEL) and the Graduate Education Loan (GEL), with the institutions acting as the lenders and MELA buying the loans from the school. To raise the funds to buy loans from the institutions, MELA issues tax-exempt bonds in the municipal market.

Since the spring of 1983, participation in the program has grown from the original nine colleges to forty-three Massachusetts institutions, including nine public institutions. To become involved, a school must sign a loan-origination agreement and commit to MELA 4 percent of the total amount of money it intends to loan.

Since December 1986, MELA has also offered a mortgage-backed option, developed in response to the changing tax laws. MELA found that, in reaction, many of their borrowers were prepaying their loans and taking out home equity loans at variable rates that were considerably higher than the rate on their MELA loan.

MELA's basic loan-processing procedure begins when a student makes an application to the school. The school then does an initial review, including a needs test, and sends the application to MELA's service representative, who completes the formal credit review on the family. If the family is approved for the loan, the promissory note returns from the servicer to the institution, and the institution deals again with the family and student. After those steps are completed, MELA buys the note from the school and transfers the money to the institution to be credited to the student's account.

Because MELA wanted to keep the second-mortgage option separate from its unsecured loans, it has arranged a two-step process for families. As a result, the system is set up so that students who apply for loans can check a box on their initial application to receive information about a secured loan. But it is only after MELA has purchased the note for that student that they send information about the program. At that point, the family can send their home mortgage information to the servicer, who completes an equity check and contracts with a separate company to conduct the title search.

If the borrower is approved for the second mortgage (or a new mortgage, if the family owns their home outright), MELA sends the family the proper mortgage forms to be completed, notarized, and returned. The servicer then hires the title company to record the mortgage in the state where the family resides.

According to MELA officials, five points are key in the administration of the mortgage-backed program.

1. *The program is structured so that neither the interest rate nor the monthly payment changes when a borrower secures the loan.* Because all home-mortgage-option borrowers start out with the first step in the two-step process—arranging for an unsecured

loan—MELA maintains the same interest rate so that the monthly payment does not change once the loan is secured.

2. *MELA has established the program in such a way that the Authority is always a junior lien holder on the secured properties.* In the majority of cases, applicants for MELA's mortgage-backed program have a first mortgage on their house held by a bank or other lending institution. Therefore, when they apply to MELA, they fill out a second-mortgage form, which automatically positions MELA next in line behind the first lien holder and any other current lien holders.

In addition, if a borrower sells the home, MELA does not require prepayment on the loan and will discharge the mortgage for a small processing fee. If the family purchases another home, they may substitute a mortgage on that new house, as long as it meets the program's guidelines.

3. *In exchange for giving MELA the mortgage on their house, borrowers receive "preference in forgiveness" as consideration from the Authority.* MELA tells its borrowers that, if at the end of the life of their bonds, MELA has paid off all its bondholders and expenses, then they will forgive their borrowers' remaining payments. Because mortgage-backed borrowers receive preference in that forgiveness, they might be forgiven six months to a year earlier than the other borrowers.

4. *MELA offers the mortgage-backed program in all but four states: Texas, Pennsylvania, New Jersey, and Michigan.* After conducting research on the applicable laws in each of the fifty states, MELA attorneys found that the statutes regulating home-mortgage activity in those four states made it difficult for MELA to offer the program.

5. *MELA contracts with Knight Tuition Payment Plans, a professional servicer located in Boston, to administrate all their loans.* For the secured loans, the servicer approves the application and contacts the title company, Infosearch, Inc., to conduct the title search and record the mortgage. The family pays a $160 fee to cover servicing, title search, and recording.

CONCLUSION

Although mortgage backing adds to the complexity of a loan program, the requirements are not so onerous as to prevent colleges and state agencies from considering providing such an option. Like any new wrinkle in student finance, however, institutions should carefully explore not only the legal requirements for offering mortgage backing, but should also consider the institutional and public policy issues.

Two programs, one at the University of Pennsylvania and the other at the Massachusetts Educational Loan Authority, have been put into place, offering mortgage-backed loans to families on a national basis. These two plans demonstrate the possibilities for a mortgage-backed option in two very different loan programs, both of which existed before implementing this new option. Although the plans have only been running for a few years, early indications are that there is strong interest from families in this loan option.

9

FINANCING
HIGHER
EDUCATION IN
A GLOBAL
ECONOMY

ANTHONY D. KNERR

I N reflecting upon the chapters of this volume, it is clear that the viewpoint of higher education is shifting from an almost entirely domestic concern to more of an international one. The reason, of course, is that our society is increasingly becoming a part of the world politic, and international economic forces have significant influences on our economy and, consequently, on higher education.

There is a surprisingly long list of current international "involvements" of colleges and universities. These include international student enrollments; foreign area academic programs and study programs in other countries; increasing numbers of foreign-trained faculty (particularly in technical disciplines); fund raising from alumni, friends, or organizations domiciled abroad; offshore captive insurance companies; foreign investment portfolios; international money managers; licensing of intellectual properties to enterprises based in other countries; collaboration of institutions in different countries on joint research endeavors; and the exploration of foreign-denominated taxable financing. Assumptions about underlying institutional economic matters are increasingly reflective of trends and concerns in the global economy, including inflation, interest rates, utility costs, and the like. Asset allocation and capital accumulation strategies also reflect larger understandings of global economic policies, trends, and considerations.

These lists are illustrative and hardly exhaustive, but they show certain contextual aspects of the "globalization" of institutions—programmatically, managerially, operationally, and financially. Indeed, we probably lack a sufficiently explicit understanding of the depth and character of the international linkages. We need to think of our institutions in global terms and evolve a more sophisticated conceptual view that incorporates an international focus within which to plan, manage, and finance our institutions. This framework should not be limited to issues such as international student marketing, foreign fund raising, foreign campus locations, more formal connections with foreign universities, networking of research library collections and other databases, and international accreditation procedures, although these may be relevant. Rather, we need to adopt a general mindset oriented toward the international economic, political, and social forces on our institutions—a mindset that considers the economics and financing of universities from a more global, less exclusively domestic, frame of reference.

___ GROWING ECONOMIC PRESSURES

The chapters of this book have yielded several conclusions about institutional finance in the global economy. The first is that there are likely to be fundamental, continuing financial pressures as a result of the underlying economics of higher education. As

William Bowen pointed out in 1968 in *The Economics of the Major Private Universities,* rising unit costs are inescapable if faculty salaries are to keep pace with wage and productivity growth elsewhere in the economy. Absent productivity gains in education, there is nothing inherent in the economic structure to prevent educational cost per unit from rising indefinitely at a compound rate, as proved by the exception: Universities kept the growth in operating costs *and* tuition charges below the rate of general inflation in the 1970s only by substantially reducing real faculty salaries—the kind of action that cannot, of course, be repeated in most decades.

The consequences of Bowen's theorem have been amply demonstrated in institutional pricing, with the corollaries of increasing tuition discounting to fund student financial aid, and off-loading tuition price increases onto public and private sector financing. This latter action has resulted in a shift in the responsibility of paying for college from the current generation to the next generation, together with an issue of capital transfer (the increased use of capital financing to fund an income stream) that has not yet been fully acknowledged or considered.[1]

It is unclear how other elements in the institutional economic equation will change over the next 10 to 20 years, but it is reasonable to assume that there will continue to be rapid real escalation in some set of institutional nonsalary expenses (such as utilities, insurance, library serials, scientific equipment, building maintenance, and construction), catch-up on deferred maintenance, expansion in the range of intellectual inquiry, increasing demands upon the university as a social institution, and "technologicalization" of the academy.

There is only so much pressure that tuition rate increases can take (or only so much burden that tuition financing can handle). While opportunities undoubtedly exist for some productivity gains in both the academic and the administrative sides, there are also limits.[2] We may discover some additional income

1. An example of this transfer is Douglas Wofford's chapter on mortgage-backed alternative student loans.
2. There are probably more opportunities than we realize, but we have already done more in improving productivity than is commonly acknowledged.

sources—technology transfer, for instance. We will continue actively to pursue fund raising, capital formation, and appeals for increased (and more predictable) government funding of research and instruction.

These constraints may require institutions to:

- Rethink the scope and character of programs.
- Reformulate institutional goals and missions.
- Confront possibly radical changes in the underlying delivery of programs and the current assumptions about productivity.
- Reformulate the public policy assumptions underlying the academy.

Another consequence of these economic forces is that public institutions may begin to look and act financially like private institutions as tuition rates increase, fund raising is emphasized, and endowments grow. Similarly, private institutions may begin to resemble public institutions as they rely increasingly on government funding. In addition, there may be further differentiation of institutional quality (both overall and with respect to particular schools and programs) on the basis of relative wealth or distinctiveness of approach or style (the clarity and appeal of a market niche).

An additional conclusion is that regardless of whether we can influence the fundamental character of the economics of higher education, we are likely to be confronted with new levels and kinds of economic volatility that will have significant consequences for higher education. As Anderson points out in Chapter 2 of this book, our domestic economy is increasingly linked to, and dependent upon, international trade, finance, and market conditions. Changes in our domestic economy may have a significant impact on other economies (and economic sectors), and vice versa. Recent stock market behavior is ample demonstration

---

This includes such steps as energy conservation and cogeneration, self-insurance and captive insurance companies, and such shared library resources as the Research Library Group.

both of the interconnectedness and the high volatility of market-places.

If and when volatility and unpredictability increase in the economy and the marketplace, institutions need to anticipate the likely results of such occurrences—even if the precise character, nature, or timing of such disturbances cannot be forecast. There will certainly be, before the end of the century, another Black Monday, insurance rate problem, cap in indirect cost recoveries, energy price hike, regional economic shift, high tech collapse, or demographic dip. It is unlikely that there will be the kind of extraordinary disequilibrium that the combination of student activism, sudden energy price increases, and higher general rates of inflation caused in the 1970s, in no small measure because university budgeting and planning is more sophisticated than it was 10 to 15 years ago. Most institutions now have a variety of contingencies, reserves, and cushions, and total institutional asset bases are relatively higher today in real dollar terms than they were in the 1970s. This is primarily because the general economic climate has been relatively benign during the 1980s.

The long view will become more important because fundamental economic pressures require balancing of immediate and future demands and pressures, and because there is every reason to anticipate that the financing of higher education will be more difficult in 20 years than it is today.

As Frank Campanella pointed out, it is far easier to identify cost pressures on universities than it is to delineate ways of financing them. Certain obvious steps have already been taken. It is not clear what other additional efforts may yield important benefits. Further, it is not certain that the "internationalization" of our economy will either make that task any easier or provide any new sets of financing alternatives. As the playing field becomes larger, management will inevitably become more complex, and the fundamental economic pressures more intense.

Bob Forrester's chapter on the interrelationships and trade-offs between equity and debt financing delineates another important issue—how best to fund necessary capital improvements for the lowest cost. That discussion suggests that we need to take a more comprehensive view of asset/liability management and be concerned about the relative efficiency of asset availability and deployment. In the same vein, Douglas Wofford's chapter on mortgage-backed alternative student loans discusses one source of capital to generate (and possibly protect) the tuition component in the stream of operating income. Wofford's argument also shows the impetus that a public policy decision—tax reform—has had on institutional finance.

Another aspect of Forrester's trade-off analysis and a similar example of public policy implications is presented in Arthur Kalita's examination of taxable financing. The need to consider taxable financing actively is, again, a function of the Tax Reform Act. Kalita shows that institutions should be cognizant of the availability and implications of taxable financing vehicles when deciding upon capital financing strategies and, more parochially, understand the relative similarities and differences between domestic and foreign taxable financing alternatives. Dan Heimowitz's discussion of credit enhancement offers sound guidance on the important practicalities of back-stopping institutional debt capacity to reduce the cost or increase the availability of externally generated capital.

William F. Massy's discussion of direct and indirect costs of research graphically illustrates the permeation of public policy considerations into the fabric of institutional affairs. His chapter recognizes that the marriage of government sponsorship and university management of research reflects both the sensitivity of the enterprise to different value interpretations (marriage partners often see the relationship in a strikingly Rashomon manner) and to changes—even moderate alterations—in financing policies and assumptions.

CONCLUSIONS

When considering the financing of higher education it is important to remember that there are several thousand colleges and universities all of which have their own rhythms, values, structures, and concerns. We should be wary, if not chary, of generalizations in view of the individualism and particularity of each institution. That caution notwithstanding, I think there are two major conclusions of the chapters in this book.

First, although we are evolving toward a more adequate conceptual model for financing universities, we are not there yet. Most major universities and colleges now take it as a given that (1) the present—as defined by an operating budget, an investment spending rule, and annual investment in physical plant renewal—will have consequences for the future; (2) such consequences need to be well understood in making decisions about the present; and (3) institutional finance is quintessentially dynamic rather than static. The internalization of this concept has beneficially changed a great deal of institutional behavior.

Larger integrated financial planning, as suggested by Massy in his 1987 article, "Making It All Work," stresses the need to look more closely at the interactions of assets and liabilities and of the balance sheet and the operating statement. Each of the discrete activities in financial management has implications that stretch far beyond it. Without looking at the whole—through an integrated perspective—we are missing important points of connection and will lack sufficient understanding of how influential individual decisions are on other aspects of the institution.

We need a more sophisticated model or conceptualization that at once delineates interrelationships between and among asset and liability components, operating statement components, and external circumstances. Such a model would incorporate a variety of submodels (such as indirect cost recovery, faculty salary cohort studies, and tuition financing models). This approach would enable us analytically to understand better the implications of present trends for the future, the opportunities and vulnerabilities of current approaches, and ways of ensuring the stability of the underlying economic structure. Describing the operating characteristics of such a model may be beyond our current skills; I strongly sense the need to be even more analytically sophisticated than we are now.

A second conclusion concerns the implications of public policy matters for the financing of higher education and how institutional (and vendor) behavior has been influenced by changing policy decisions. The Tax Reform Act, successful efforts by institutions to persuade state legislatures to finance "economic development" projects, exploration of taxing endowment earnings, review of the unrelated business income tax, removal of mandatory retirement after a seven-year grace period for faculty, the exclusivity of proprietary ownership of intellectual property, A-21—the list goes on and on—are all examples of how government initiative is shaping the character and contours of our institutions. Such government involvement will not abate: As the financial pressures on universities increase—because of both the fundamental economics of higher education and the influence of external factors—the government will become more and more involved in the very fabric of institutional financing and support, sometimes in ways we will appreciate, at other times in ways we abhor.

The other side of this public policy coin is increased interest in education matters by the public at large. Such issues as curricular reform, the role of liberal arts education in a technological world, the question of business ethics, the lack of literate, thoughtful, well-trained manpower, the importance of basic research to economic competitiveness, and the cost of education are high on the public agenda.

There are other reasons for the emerging exposure of universities in the public policy areas. On the one hand, we have perhaps been too successful in capital formation in recent years. Billion- and multibillion-dollar endowments suggest a financial healthiness that in the public mind—or at least in the government mind—may be too robust. Rapid growth in endowment size during a period when tuition rate increases were substantially above the rate of inflation produced a serious vulnerability. Higher education has not done a good job in explaining why it costs as much as it does to earn a B.A. or M.B.A. And with tuition rate increases being increasingly funded by personal borrowing—through government loans or private source financing—and by personal savings, there is a significant "hidden" form of capital transfer, the public policy implications of which need to be carefully considered.

On the other hand, our aggressive efforts to market intellectual property—and our efforts to expand income in general through such steps as real estate development, retail bookstores, and the like—mean we are entering new marketplaces in nontraditional ways, thereby raising public policy questions about what kind of public support we deserve.

It may very well be that we are at a major point of transition—that the conceptual models of the past are no longer adequate to shape appropriately the public policy considerations necessary for our future. This at the very time our society is trying to find a new conceptual framework for larger political and economic concerns.

In any case, we clearly do not have a coherent national policy on higher education and we are wavering back and forth, or being jerked back and forth, both because of the complexity of our times and because of our failure to develop and articulate a point of view. We in the academy should take several steps:

- We need to do a better job of explaining the importance of higher education to our society and the value of the social and personal investment in our institutions.
- We need to be more forceful (and effective) advocates for longer-term perspectives and shared sets of assumptions that would guide us for the next few decades.
- We need to be even more aware than we are now of the vulnerabilities that changing public policy considerations may bring.
- We need to plan for the inevitable economic shocks that will come to the economy and, ultimately, reverberate through our system of colleges and universities.

143

BIBLIOGRAPHY

Academy Industry Program, Government-University-Industry Research Roundtable. (1986) *New Alliances and Partnerships in American Science and Engineering.* Washington, DC: National Academy Press.

Anderson, Charles A. (1985) "Conditions Affecting College and University Financial Strength." *Higher Education Panel Report No. 63.* Washington, DC: American Council on Education.

Anderson, Richard E. (1988) "The Economy and Higher Education." *Capital Ideas* 3, no. 1 [entire issue]. New York: Forum for College Financing.

Anderson, Richard E., and Joel W. Meyerson, eds. (1987) *Financing Higher Education: Strategies After Tax Reform.* San Francisco: Jossey-Bass.

Association of American Universities. (1980) *The Scientific Instrumentation Needs of Research Universities.* Washington, DC: A Report to the National Science Foundation.

Association of Governing Boards. (1985) *Financial Responsibilities of Governing Boards.* Washington, DC: Association of Governing Boards.

Bartlett, J. W., and J. V. Siena. (1984) "Research and Development Limited Partnerships as a Device to Exploit University Owned Technology." *Journal of College and University Law* 10:435.

145

Bergsten, Fred C., and William R. Cline. (1985) *The United States-Japan Economic Problem.* Washington, DC: Institute for International Economics.

Bowen, Howard R. (1980) *The Costs of Higher Education.* San Francisco: Jossey-Bass.

Bowen, William G. (1968) *The Economics of the Major Private Universities.* Berkeley, CA: Carnegie Commission on the Future of Higher Education.

Bruggeman, William B., and Leo D. Stone. (1981) *Real Estate Finance.* 7th ed. Homewood, IL: Richard D. Irwin.

Callen, Patrick M., ed. (1986) "Environmental Scanning for Strategic Leadership." *New Directions for Institutional Research No. 52.* San Francisco: Jossey-Bass.

Chaffee, Ellen Earle. (1983) *Rational Decision Making in Higher Education.* Boulder, CO: National Center for Higher Education Management Systems.

Clapp, David C. (1987) "Tax Reform and the Bond Market." In *Financing Higher Education: Strategies After Tax Reform,* Anderson and Meyerson, eds. San Francisco: Jossey-Bass.

Clarke, Marianne K. (1986) *Revitalizing State Economies: A Review of State Economic Development Policies and Programs.* Washington, DC: National Governors Association.

Cohen, Stephen S., and John Zysman. (1987) *Manufacturing Matters: The Myth of the Post-Industrial Economy.* New York: Basic Books.

Committee for Economic Development. (1986) *Leadership for Dynamic State Economies.* New York: Committee for Economic Development.

Dickmeyer, Nathan. (1983) *Financial Conditions of Colleges and Universities.* Washington, DC: NACUBO.

Economic Report of the President. (1988) Washington, DC: U.S. Government Printing Office.

Eden, C. Gregory H. (1987) "Tax Exempt Leasing for Colleges and Universities." *In Financing Higher Education: Strategies After Tax Reform,* Anderson and Meyerson, eds. San Francisco: Jossey-Bass.

"Equipment Financing Ideas." (1986) *Capital Ideas* 1, no. 2 [entire issue]. New York: Forum for College Financing.

Financing and Managing University Research Equipment. (1985) Report of the AAU, NASULGC, and COGGR, Washington, DC.

Foose, Robert A., and Joel W. Meyerson. (1986) *Alternative Approaches to Tuition Financing: Making Tuition More Affordable.* Washington, DC: NACUBO.

Forrester, Robert. (1988) *Handbook on Debt Management for Colleges and Universities.* Washington, DC: NACUBO.

Fosler, R. Scott. (1988) *The New Economic Role of American States: Strategies in a Competitive World Economy.* New York: Oxford University Press.

Franck, Gail F., Richard E. Anderson, and Clark Bernard. (1987) "Tax Reform and Higher Education." In *Financing Higher Education: Strategies After Tax Reform,* Anderson and Meyerson, eds. San Francisco: Jossey-Bass.

Friedman, Benjamin M. (1988) *Day of Reckoning: The Consequences of American Economic Policy Under Reagan and After.* New York: Random House.

Goldstein, Michael B. (1987) "Equity Financing: Research Partnerships." In *Financing Higher Education: Strategies After Tax Reform*, Anderson and Meyerson, eds. San Francisco: Jossey-Bass.

Halpern, David P. (1987) *The State of College and University Facilities: A Survey of College and University Planners.* Ann Arbor, MI.: The Society for College and University Planning/University of Michigan.

Heskett, James L. (1986) *Managing in the Service Economy.* Boston: Harvard Business School Press.

Hennigan, Patrick J. "Capital Financing for Higher Education." *J.P. Morgan Report*, September 1988.

"Higher Education Passes Test for Now." *Standard and Poor's Credit Week*, September 1988.

Hopkins, David S.P., and William F. Massy. (1981) *Planning Models for Colleges and Universities.* Stanford, CA: Stanford University Press

Hyatt, James A. (1980) *A Cost Accounting Handbook for Colleges and Universities.* Washington, DC: NACUBO.

Hyatt, James A., and Aurora Santiago. (1986) *Financial Management of Colleges and Universities.* Washington, DC: NACUBO.

Internal Revenue Code of 1986. Vol. 1. Chicago: Commerce Clearing House.

Kaiser, Harvey H. (1987) "Capital Needs in Higher Education." In *Financing Higher Education: Strategies After Tax Reform*, Anderson and Meyerson, eds. San Francisco: Jossey-Bass.

King, George A. (1988) "Rethinking Higher Education Capital Finance." *Capital Ideas* 3, nos. 2 & 3 [entire issues]. New York: Forum for College Financing.

Komar, Joseph A. (1989) "Distributed Computing by Opportunity (Not Plan)." *EDUTECH Report* 4, no. 11.

Litan, Robert E., Robert Z. Lawrence, and Charles L. Schultze, eds. (1988) *American Living Standards: Threats and Challenges.* Washington, DC: The Brookings Institution.

Madsen, Claudina, and John H. Walker. (1983) *Risk Management and Insurance: A Handbook of Fundamentals.* Washington, DC: NACUBO.

Marris, Stephan. (1985) *Deficits and the Dollar: The World Economy at Risk.* Washington, DC: Institute for International Economics.

Massy, William F. (1987) "Making It All Work: Sound Financial Management." In *Financing Higher Education: Strategies After Tax Reform,* Anderson and Meyerson, eds. San Francisco: Jossey-Bass.

"Mortgage Backed Student Loans." (1987) *Capital Ideas* 2, no. 2 [entire issue]. New York: Forum for College Financing.

National Academy of Sciences. (1983) *Strengthening the Government-University Partnership in Science.* Washington DC: National Academy Press.

"New Approaches to Debt Financing." (1987) *Capital Ideas* 2, no. 1 [entire issue]. New York: Forum for College Financing.

Report of the SJR 90 Joint Subcommittee on Methods of Financing Replacement of Obsolete or Unusable Equipment in Institutions of Higher Education. (1986) Commonwealth of Virginia, Richmond.

"Tax Reform and Higher Education." (1986) *Capital Ideas* 1, nos. 3 & 4 [entire issues]. New York: Forum for College Financing.

Thomas, Richard, and Jonathan Davies. (1987) "Equity Financing: Real Estate." In *Financing Higher Education: Strategies After Tax Reform*, Anderson and Meyerson, eds. San Francisco: Jossey-Bass.

U.S. General Accounting Office. (1984) *Studies of U.S. Universities' Research Equipment Needs Inconclusive.* Washington, DC.

U.S. Supreme Court. (1988) *State of South Carolina* v. *James A. Baker III.* Supreme Court of the U.S., 485 U.S. 505; 108 S. Ct. 1355.

Welzenbach, Lenora F., ed. (1982) *College and University Business Administration.* Washington, DC: NACUBO.

INDEX